Images of the Southern Writer

# Images of the Southern Writer

Photographs by Mark Morrow

The University of Georgia Press  Athens

© 1985 by the University of Georgia Press
Athens, Georgia 30602

Designed by Sandra Strother Hudson
Set in ten on thirteen Century Old Style
The paper in this book meets the guidelines for
permanence and durability of the Committee on
Production Guidelines for Book Longevity of the
Council on Library Resources.

Printed in the United States of America

89  88  87  86  85    5  4  3  2  1

Library of Congress Cataloging in Publication Data

Morrow, Mark.
    Images of the Southern writer.

    1. Authors, American—Southern States—Portraits.
2. Authors, American—20th century—Portraits.
I. Title.
PS261.M67  1986      810′.9′975        85-8629
ISBN 0-8203-0810-2

For my parents, who loved me,
And for Patrice, who wouldn't let me give up.

# Foreword

Many writers attempt to give new meanings to old words. This is an admirable undertaking and it does invigorate all manner of poetry and prose. However, Southern writers, perhaps more successfully than any others, have infused their wordage with timeless implications. As a result, critics and readers in other regions of America sometimes are led to believe that a Southern school of writing actually exists somewhere in the Deep South and that only native-born Southerners are privileged to enroll and be nurtured by its tutelage.

When called upon to offer proof of the existence of such an institution, the best that can be done by the observers is to cite the prevalence of the ubiquitous Southern accent and the often incomprehensible pronunciation by Southerners of words of common usage.

Southern readers themselves have no such misconception. Everyone of the kind is familiar with the telltale visage of the genuine Southern writer and accepts him without doubt as being a member of the clan. These are the fellow countrymen who claim it is easy to identify a person as either being or not being a Southern writer merely by a close inspection of a photograph. And there are other experts who make claim that they can positively identify a writer as being Southern-born by finding in his photograph unmistakable evidence that he was raised on hominy grits and redeye gravy, fried apples and spoon bread.

Mark Morrow's gallery of portraits of Southern writers offers the opportunity for people everywhere to engage in the fascinating search for revealing signs and symbols of Southern cookery in American literature.

ERSKINE CALDWELL

vii

# Introduction

Southern writers have, as a group, been almost as skittish about having their pictures taken as they have been about being thought of as Southern writers. More often than not they have relented only when prodded—and then because publishing ritual dictates that authors' photographs appear on dust jackets. Flannery O'Connor, for example, told a friend that she hated "like sin" to have her picture taken, and when her first book was published she wrote her publisher that she liked everything about it "except meeting myself in that thunderclap fashion on the back of the jacket."

One noteworthy exception was William Faulkner, the reclusive Mississippi writer who, paradoxically, seems to have been ready to pose at the appearance of a camera and who had his friend "Colonel" J. R. Cofield, just off the town square, as his photographer-in-residence.

In general, the degree to which these writers were sought after by photographers—or by magazines which commanded photographers—is an index to the size of their literary reputations, a fact that in the last years of O'Connor's life brought them to the doorstep of her Georgia home in increasing numbers. Likewise, Eudora Welty, once the secret treasure of the critics and the cognoscenti, had by the eighties achieved celebrity status and the burdens that come with it—one of those burdens being requests to have her photograph taken.

But until I headed out of Columbia, South Carolina, in the fall of 1979 on the first of many such trips, no photographer—as far as I know—had taken it upon himself or herself to go among the herd (or pride?) of Southern writers and catch them as they were one moment in the late years of the twentieth century. My project would eventually span five years, and several of my intended subjects would die before they could sit for me; several others who sat for me died before the book came to be published.

Even after going among them I cannot explain why Southerners are good storytellers and why the South has consistently produced good and sometimes great writers. Some have suggested that the Southern storytelling tradition came from the South's predominantly rural character and the absence of large urban centers. I do know that the storytelling tradition existed when I grew up with the baby-boom generation in Greer, South Carolina, a small farm and cotton mill town near Greenville, and that it still exists today despite the growth of urban areas like Atlanta, Charlotte, Nashville, and Richmond.

I am not an academic, but I like to read and I like to talk about books. This fact was not lost on the writers I photographed over the last five years. Most said, "You're the first photographer I've ever met who's actually read my books." They made it sound as if reading had been a hard pill to swallow. The pleasure of reading Walker

Percy, Anne Tyler, Madison Jones, Robert Penn Warren, Eudora Welty, Ernest Gaines, Barry Hannah, or any other of the forty-eight writers was exactly the reason I kept taking pictures.

Many writers invited me into their homes, fed me, got out their best bourbon, and told me their best stories. Welty, against her better judgment, allowed me to photograph her in a hallway and in a chair that she told me she never used "except when I talk on the phone, and I associate it with nothing but resignation and impatience." I cannot be egocentric enough to believe they were trying to put their best foot forward for an unknown photographer without contract, money, or professional-looking equipment.

Several of the writers who agreed to be photographed for inclusion in this volume on Southern writers did so while protesting the label. A Southern writer, by my definition, is a writer who was born in the South or who was brought up there—who spent his or her formative years in one of the thirteen states that I have decided to call Southern: Louisiana, Mississippi, Arkansas, Tennessee, Kentucky, Texas, Florida, Alabama, Georgia, South Carolina, North Carolina, Virginia, and West Virginia. A Southern writer, by my definition, uses Southern characters and settings in his/her books or has strong fictional Southern ties to his/her characters.

For the purposes of this book, the author also had to be a *serious* novelist, short story writer, poet, or playwright—which eliminated entirely the supermarket novels with the "tinfoil writing on the cover and women in long dresses," as North Carolina writer Sylvia Wilkinson describes the genre.

My one regret is that I could not photograph everyone who deserves recognition. Some writers declined to be photographed; others could not easily be reached. And the simple fact is that there was not enough money—and ultimately not enough time. A recent book lists 434 Southern writers who published novels between 1940 and 1983. This project could have gone on forever.

Images of the Southern Writer

# A. R. Ammons

A. R. Ammons didn't much look like a poet coming down the grand staircase of the Reynolda House in Winston-Salem, North Carolina. Poets are supposed to look haggard and concerned. Ammons reminded me more of a high school chemistry teacher than a National Book Award-winning poet (*Collected Poems, 1951–1971*) and the author of seventeen other books. But there he was, sweeping past Ming Dynasty vases, Chippendale furniture, and Brussels tapestries with a sunglasses case in his pocket that at first resembled a plastic penholder of the variety automotive parts salesmen sport.

Ammons is a friendly man who doesn't seem much removed from his Whiteville, North Carolina, beginnings. He attended Wake Forest University and was for a time principal at a small school on Cape Hatteras. Although he left the South in 1951 to attend the University of California at Berkeley and has taught at Cornell since 1964, his poems still reflect his rural North Carolina background. Says Ammons, "I'm still, in some internal way, a Southern writer."

Ammons had come to North Carolina from his home in Ithaca, New York, to give a reading at the former home (now a museum) of R. J. Reynolds Tobacco Company founder Joshua Reynolds. He pulled out a set of keys when we sat down in the grand living room and began fiddling with them. "Well, anyway, I'm glad you could meet me here," he said, smiling. "Ithaca is not on the way to anywhere."

Ammons had brought along some of his paintings, and we decided to try them as a background, but a group of touring fourth-grade children foiled that idea. The only deserted place seemed to be the elegant indoor pool, but the thick glass covering made the temperature unbearable. Ammons wiped a drop of perspiration from his forehead. "How about a picture of a poet diving into a pool?" he said, laughing.

Inside, the visitors had finished their tour. I noticed a painting that seemed to suit a poet who is often associated with Robert Frost and Wallace Stevens. I didn't know the painting was a Thomas Hart Benton called *Bootleggers*.

Ammons thought the idea of posing in front of the painting humorous. He laughed and playfully struck poses. Later, sitting on the sun porch adjacent to the grand living room, he looked over to the Benton painting and said with a laugh, "Why don't you just tell your editors that this is Archie Ammons posing in front of one of his more famous paintings?"

# Doris Betts

"I'm a very hard person to photograph," Doris Betts was saying, brushing her prize Arabian horse, Sockdolager, at her farm in Pittsboro, North Carolina. "I think it's instinctive, you know, the belief that the black box does take your soul away." She grabbed my arm and her laugh echoed off the little farmhouse and the large barn where she keeps her other Arabians.

Betts and her husband Lowry, an attorney who now devotes full time to the horses, have so many Arabians that she had to think a few seconds to decide whether they had thirteen or fourteen horses. It was a cool spring morning and she mounted her favorite horse easily and rode around the large pasture. "Not bad for someone who didn't even learn to ride until she was fifty," she said with a smile, opening the gate to walk the horse back to the barn.

Betts, who has been publishing steadily since she won the *Mademoiselle* college fiction prize when she was a sophomore in college, was working on her fourth novel, *Heading West* (1982). I asked her how she found time to write between raising horses, teaching at Chapel Hill, and posing for insistent photographers. "You can't bother me," she said, scoffing at the idea of intruding on her work. "I don't have any schedule. I'm a pick-up and put-down writer. I write in bits and snatches. Besides, I welcome any excuses to do something else other than writing."

After she had stabled the horse, she introduced me to her other Arabians down the length of the long barn. Then we walked back to the house and sat in her study, which is also the living room, and I asked her if she liked living in Pittsboro. "Sure," she said, throwing one of her several cats off her lap. "I've always said that if I ever lived any place else it would be some place like Durango, Colorado. But I like living here because it's near my material and the people I know the best."

"Does that make you a Southern writer?" I ventured. Betts said she supposed it did. "But I question whether the term fits any more," she added. "What does Pittsboro have in common with Atlanta? Atlanta is more like Philadelphia or Chicago now. Besides, the stereotypes don't fit any more. Some people still think that because you speak slowly, you think slowly. Which is not exactly true, is it?" Betts said with a smile, looking at the room full of books around her.

# Erskine Caldwell

Erskine Caldwell was standing in front of a portrait of himself as a young man sitting amidst stacks of books balancing a typewriter on his lap. In the painting he is looking intently out of the canvas, his chin cupped in his right hand while a host of his fictional characters dance about the background. Caldwell swung a thumb back toward the painting. "Fairly handsome guy, don't you think?" he said, laughing.

Although the painting was of a man thirty years younger, Caldwell had lost none of the energy and enthusiasm captured by the artist. He was a man who still wrote every day, published books, and made no apologies for his life or his work.

Caldwell is a legendary figure in American literature. His first two books, *Tobacco Road* (1932) and *God's Little Acre* (1933), brought as much criticism as praise. Both were called obscene by decency leagues of the day and criticized because they exaggerated the deprivation of the post-Depression South. But, despite the criticism, the two novels sold seventeen million copies and helped realign America's literary tastes. The court case that followed the publication of Caldwell's novels helped set a precedent for other controversial works like James Joyce's *Ulysses* and Henry Miller's *Tropic of Cancer.*

"Critics," he said later, sitting by the pool at his home in Scottsdale, Arizona, "I don't pay any attention to them." Caldwell is well aware of his legendary status. "My publisher gets letters all the time asking whether I'm still alive," he said, laughing, "but I assure you I'm quite alive." Even Caldwell's stationery attests to the grit and the hard-nosed attitude of the man. Across the top in script it says, "Illegitimi Non Carborundum," which, loosely translated, means "Don't let the bastards get you down."

Caldwell is also pretty hard-nosed on the subject of how one becomes a successful writer, even in today's competitive market. "Success is easy if you want it bad enough," he told me. "If you're not successful as a writer, then it's your own fault, not the editors', publishers', or reading public's."

Caldwell was born in Georgia, the son of a Presbyterian minister. His career took him to Atlanta as a $25-a-week reporter, to New York, and then to Maine, where for seven years he tried to make it as a writer. He was in Hollywood for five years as a scriptwriter before going to Russia as a reporter for *Life* magazine and CBS radio in 1941. He even collaborated with the great photographer Margaret Bourke-White, the second of his four wives, on books about prewar Czechoslovakia, wartime Russia, and his native South.

I asked Caldwell if he had any favorite writers. "I don't admire anybody but myself," he said. "I don't read other writers, so I don't know who's great. Robert Penn Warren is an extremely good writer. He can do anything, but if he concentrated on one thing he'd be Superman." He thought for a moment and then added, laughing, "Hell, he's probably a musician for all I know. Maybe he plays the saxophone."

# Fred Chappell

Drummond, Fred Chappell's cat, watched his owner being photographed with a cat's halfhearted interest and eventually sauntered out of the room in search of a more noble pastime. "I guess we're ailurophiles," Chappell said, watching his cat leave the room, "even if they're not androphiles." He took a sip of coffee from his cup, which was decorated with cats leapfrogging over one another, and lit another cigarette. Chappell seemed to be a man perfectly content with himself and his art.

"It's an awful thing to say," he told me in his slow but precise Southern accent, "and it's probably bad luck to say so, but if I had to tell the truth I'd say that I was very happy." He laughed and looked over to his wife Susan, who had entered the room carrying the cat.

Chappell, who published the first of his twelve books while still a graduate student, is considered by many critics to be one of the best of the Southern-born writers. Yet, like the early Faulkner, he has not received as much attention in America as he has in Europe. The lack of popular acclaim and the money it brings does not seem to bother him,

however. "If I had more money," Chappell said, crossing his legs and leaning forward to ponder the question, "I'd just have to give it away to charity, which would get me in all kinds of tax trouble. . . . Besides," he added, a smile crossing his face, "I know that money is not going to make me happier, or wiser, and certainly not better-looking. Hell, you can't get better-looking than me."

Chappell lives in a modest home near the University of North Carolina–Greensboro campus where he is writer-in-residence. He says he likes teaching because it allows him the freedom to write what he pleases without worrying about marketability. "I think people should do exactly as they please as long as they don't harm somebody else, and if people would rather read somebody else's books than mine, then I don't see it hurts a thing in the world. Besides, you have to remember that books which are big commercial successes pay for those of us who are not."

The phone rang and Chappell asked his wife to answer it. He said he hated the phone—not because he gets so many calls from fans or aspiring novelists who want him to read 600-page manuscripts, but because he cannot say no. "There's something about a disembodied voice that gets me every time," he said. "I don't even dare answer the phone unless I know who it is. Salesmen call me up asking me to come look at condominiums or mountain chalets and I always agree to go. Of course, I never show up."

# Brainard Cheney

Brainard Cheney—Lon to his friends—poured a stiff drink of bourbon from a half-full Very Old Barton bottle and handed it to me. He poured himself a healthy scotch and sat down with great ease and flexibility for a man of eighty-two, crossing one leg over the other. "I wish I could still drink bourbon. I prefer it," he said, holding his glass with both hands, "but I developed an allergy to bourbon and it gave me headaches, so I had to switch to scotch, but until then I lived very well on it."

Cheney, who lives in Smyrna, Tennessee, in a house built as the Civil War was ending, spent most of his career as a political writer for the *Nashville Banner*. He published his first novel, *Lightwood,* in 1939, and his last in 1969. Lately Cheney has been working on his memoirs, which most likely will include a few chapters about the visitors to Idlers' Retreat, the name given the Cheneys' home by its original owners in the 1870s.

The guest list at Idlers' Retreat reads like a who's who of Southern writers. Robert Penn Warren, Eudora Welty, Allen Tate, Flannery O'Connor, Caroline Gordon, and Andrew Lytle were just a few of the frequent guests. O'Connor even had her own room downstairs because of the pain she experienced climbing stairs. Sometimes several writers would visit at once, Cheney said. "But we didn't have a seminar or anything like that. We did talk about our work in progress on occasion. Red Warren was responsible for my writing novels rather than short stories," he said. "Red told me short stories were hard to sell and you never get paid enough. Besides, he told me you can make more of an impression with a novel." Later, Cheney was able to help Warren when he was working on *All the King's Men.* "I was working as a political writer and so Red used to ask me about the court system and politics. I also advised him on how an electric chair worked."

But of all the famous writers who visited Idlers' Retreat, Cheney said, Eudora Welty was among his favorites. "I tell you," he said, laughing with the memory, "she was just about the funniest girl I have ever met."

# John William Corrington

John William Corrington was sitting out by his pool with the first 1,200 pages of his novel *The Man Who Slept with Women* in his lap and a cigar in his mouth. The novel, later retitled *Shad Sentell,* was the third in an as-yet-incomplete trilogy that began with Corrington's first novel, *And Wait for the Night,* published in 1964. Corrington dumped the manuscript out of his lap and told me to come through the back gate of his New Orleans home off fashionable St. Charles Avenue. "You should have brought your bathing suit," he said, sitting back down again under the shade of a poolside umbrella.

Corrington, whose first book was a collection of poems that won the Charioteer Poetry Prize, is a writer hard to classify. He holds a doctor of philosophy degree in English and American studies from the University of Sussex and a law degree from Tulane University. He was a practicing lawyer until 1978 when he and his wife Joyce, a former chemistry professor at Xavier University in New Orleans, began new careers as head writers for the daytime soap *Search for Tomorrow.* They have since been writers of *Texas* and *General Hospital* and have written a fair number of feature motion pictures.

Although it is unusual for a television writer to live so far away from the set, Corrington manages to get around the distance via express mail, the telephone, and a home computer. "The last job we had," he said, "they were determined we were going to pick up, sell the house, and move to New York, and I said, 'You ain't got that kind of money.'"

Corrington, who doesn't mind admitting his pride in his Southern heritage, said he wouldn't think of living any place other than New Orleans, except his hometown of Shreveport. Coming from that part of Louisiana gives his persona a Western twist, he said—hence his comfort with cowboy boots and hats. But that's where persona ends. Corrington is a voracious reader who has an amazing ability to marshal facts. A conversation with him on almost any subject can be a humbling experience.

He scoffs at those who would criticize his work and his loyalty to the South. "I never fool with writers," he said. "My associates are mostly lawyers and a few academics. There's still this romantic illusion in America that says you must wrestle with the demons of your soul and that a great novel takes ten or twenty years to write," Corrington said, taking a puff on his cigar. "I say that's baloney. Where I come from, they say, 'If you think long, you think wrong.'"

# Harry Crews

Harry Crews shouted at his German shepherd barking behind the redwood fence that surrounded his home in Gainesville, Florida. "Why the hell don't you shut up?" he said gruffly. The dog obediently obliged his master's command and sat down.

Crews, who has a reputation as a tough character, does in fact look the part. He is a large man who looks you in the eye as if looking for signs of weakness. But looks can be deceiving. Although Crews probably wouldn't mind reaching across a barroom table to grab a collar if the need arose, he is an amiable writer who likes to tell a good story.

When *The Gospel Singer,* his first book, was published in 1968, critics called the thirty-four-year-old writer "promising," but had reservations about his sometimes grotesque and horrifying novel. Crews is aware of the criticism, but he said those critics haven't taken a close enough look at his books. "I have a hell of a lot of empathy for those people," he said, sitting in his backyard, thick with pine and tropical plants. "I can say a lot more about what the world calls normal by writing about what it calls abnormal."

Crews's fiction is a product of what the young author saw and experienced growing up. In his 1978 autobiography, *A Childhood,* Crews tells about growing up in poverty-stricken Bacon County, Georgia. "My daddy died before I was old enough to remember him," he said, "and my momma married his brother. We lived on a series of tenant farms where you could lie awake at night and look through the roof and see the stars. I grew up on a steady diet of biscuits made with lard and water and no milk."

Crews said he got out of Georgia by joining the Marines at seventeen. A picture of him hanging on his wall attests to the man he says was "lean, mean, and ready for anything." After three years in the Marines he went to the University of Florida and studied under Andrew Lytle, eventually getting a master's degree in education. Crews said he worked ten years at writing before he sold anything. He said his unpublished first novel was "mechanical, unreadable," but it was an important learning experience.

Crews, who has been involved in numerous bodily abuses, told me he'd managed to break just about every major bone from either brawls or motor vehicle accidents. He told a particularly rambunctious story about how he had gotten a good deal of money from the sale of an article and vowed to spend it one night on the coast of Florida. "And we almost did it," he said, smiling, "except this guy picked a fight with us and we got thrown in jail. But at least it was a Florida jail. I like those the best," Crews said.

# James Dickey

"Do you want to play guitar," James Dickey asked me in his distinctive, often imitated accent, "or do you want to go ahead and take some pictures?"

We sat down and he picked up one of the three Martin guitars resting on stands in his 10,000-volume library and handed it to me. He picked up a 12-string and executed fine flat picking and Travis picking while I followed along. "You ever had any fantasy about being a musician?" I asked.

"No," he said, shaking his head, "I like the musician situation, but I never wanted to be a musician. I didn't really play a lot until I was forty. That makes over twenty years, and you ought to be able to play something in all that time."

Dickey, a Columbia, South Carolina, resident for the past twenty years, is a poet famous not only for his poetry but also for a popular novel and movie, *Deliverance* (1970). The book and subsequent movie were so popular that many people don't seem to know the name James Dickey unless "author of *Deliverance*" is added parenthetically. Does it bother a National Book Award-winning poet to be remembered that way? I asked him.

"There are many writers who'd give a good deal to have something like *Deliverance* happen to them," he said, sitting now in front of his sextants and plotting equipment. "If I have readers here and there and they're the ones I want, or the ones I want when I'm dead, then that's enough for me."

Dickey, who is a rated navigator and avid stargazer, held up one of his sextants and looked at it as if admiring a fine work of art. "Star observation," he said, explaining his interest, "arouses religious feelings in a lot of people and I'm not sure it doesn't in me. I remember watching the transit of Saturn for the first time. There it was—sitting out there in that absolute silent space. I said, this is for me."

*Alnilam,* a novel that Dickey has been working on for years, has much to do with his interest in star observation and flying. "What I want to do," he told me, "is to restore the sense of flight to flying. It can only be felt now in very light planes. It's really a godlike point of view. If you ever see a city like New York from the air at night, it doesn't look like a city, but a vision of a city."

Back in Dickey's study, he showed me the bow Burt Reynolds used in *Deliverance*. Although he doesn't claim to be an actor, Dickey played a cracker sheriff in the movie. With a little coaxing from me, he delivered his memorable advice to the battered and exhausted Jon Voight, cracker accent and all.

"Don't you all come back up here again," he said, looking me squarely in the eyes. "Don't you all do nothing like this again."

# Ellen Douglas

Ellen Douglas said she began writing as a DJ during World War II. "We had these huge eighteen-inch platters," she said, sitting in her Greenville, Mississippi, home, "and they played for twenty-seven minutes. It was like being a fireman. Unless there's a fire, you don't have anything to do. I'd just put on the record and then I'd have twenty-five minutes to write before I had an advertisement to read."

Douglas said that her writing at the radio station was confined to short stories, but that some of the stories eventually became part of her 1962 novel *A Family's Affairs*. Although working for a radio station was fun, she said, she never intended to be a journalist. "Radio was just a job. I never wanted to be an announcer."

Douglas, who now lives in Jackson and teaches at the University of Mississippi in Oxford, didn't publish her first novel until she was forty-one.

The story of how she got *A Family's Affairs* published is a long tale of a writer-acquaintance who had an editor-friend who liked her book and entered it in a contest.

"It sounds like a lot of luck," Douglas was quick to add, "but I had been working on that novel for six years. It's like a rock-and-roll star who pops out of nowhere and then you find out he's been working like a dog since he was fifteen."

Greenville is a town with a literary legacy. William Alexander Percy, author of *Lanterns on the Levee*, Walker Percy, Charles G. Bell, and Shelby Foote were all born in Greenville or grew up there. When Douglas moved there in 1946, Foote was living there, "reading through the canon of English literature chronologically," Douglas said.

"He was a wonderful companion," she said. "We used to read plays aloud. We had a group that read Shakespeare all one winter. Shelby even had a book that had an indexing system so you could assign parts and no one would ever end up talking to himself."

Douglas told me she was a sixth- or seventh-generation Mississippian. She said her family came to the Natchez area before the Revolutionary War. "My family's a mixed bag. All those folks married one another, you know. One was in the Spanish service. Some were very pious Presbyterians and others Catholic. But," she said, laughing, "I think the Presbyterians won out."

# Charles Edward Eaton

When Charles Edward Eaton was in his early twenties, Robert Frost wrote one of his rare letters and told him he'd been awarded the Robert Frost Fellowship to Breadloaf. Eaton, who had studied under Frost at Harvard, said he "nearly jumped through the roof" when he got the letter. "He really started me on my literary career."

Later, when Eaton was teaching creative writing at Chapel Hill, where he now lives, Frost visited his classes every year. "Everybody always says what a so-and-so he was," Eaton said in his mellifluous Southern voice, "but he could be a very generous man if he liked you and your work."

Eaton, who was born in Winston-Salem, North Carolina, has published nine volumes of poetry, three collections of short stories, and a book of art criticism. Although he has won the Ridgely Torrence Memorial Award, the Golden Rose from the New England Poetry Club, the Alice Fay di Castagnola Award of $3,500, and an O. Henry Award for the short story, among others, he does not believe "literary achievement should be equated with winning awards." Asked about his nomination for a National Book Award for his third collection, *The Greenhouse in the Garden,* he said, "Who knows what effect winning it might have had? Sometimes success of this sort can ruin a writer once the publicity machine gets going. It's what finally happens to your work that's important, isn't it?"

Although Eaton spent the first part of his life in the environments of the University of North Carolina, Princeton, and Harvard, he has never been a strict academician. Establishing a lifelong pattern of balancing intellectual pursuit with experience, he spent a year in Puerto Rico followed by four years in Brazil as vice-consul at the embassy in Rio de Janeiro which yielded material for three books. "I have always thought of my life," he said, "as a continuing odyssey of education and art."

He and his wife Isabel have an extensive collection of American paintings and in 1973 organized a national retrospective of Karl Knaths which was circulated by International Exhibitions Foundation. Eaton, whose mother was a painter, said, "Painting has been the second most important influence on my work."

"Any artist has a pretty tough time in America," Eaton told me, sitting in front of a painting by Robert Beauchamp, "whether it's money or getting recognition. An artist must believe in what he's doing even if, like Herman Melville, you only sell five hundred copies of *Moby-Dick* or, like Walt Whitman, you have to sell your poems out of a basket. You must go ahead with your work even if it's not recognized, or you'll be a totally frustrated human being." Eaton thought a moment, trying to put a Yeats quote together. "Be secret and exult," he said finally, "because of all things known, that is most difficult."

# Shelby Foote

Shelby Foote is a Southerner and doesn't mind being called one. "It's silly," he said, "to resent being called a Southern writer. It doesn't mean any more than saying you're a New York or a New Hampshire writer."

Foote was born in Greenville, Mississippi, and grew up with his friend Walker Percy in what he considered an ideal environment, a small Southern community. "We have a tendency to overrate our past experiences," he said, "but growing up in Greenville was a great experience. A town of fifteen thousand people and everybody knew everybody and you got a chance to see all segments of society instead of just the rich or the poor."

Foote moved to Memphis in 1953 because he wanted to stay in the Mississippi Delta and "Memphis is the capital of the Delta." Although he was asked on several occasions to write screenplays in Hollywood, once by Stanley Kubrick, he always declined. "The temptations are just too great out there with all the booze and women. I'd probably go crazy."

Foote, who has written six novels, his last *September, September* (1978), is perhaps best known for his definitive history of the Civil War called *The Civil War: A Narrative,* a three-volume work which he began in 1954 and which took twenty years to complete. He was awarded three Guggenheim fellowships to work on those volumes.

A good portion of one wall in his study is lined with beautifully bound longhand copies of his work. Each page is a work of art, a series of eloquent lines centered exactly on paper that has the feel and crackle of parchment. Foote said the practice of writing exclusively with dip-pen and acid-free paper is just a hobby. "I took a German course at Chapel Hill," he said, picking out a book, "and got interested in calligraphy by looking at the old German script, but I never took any classes." When he quits writing for the day, he makes a copy of his work and then types from that copy.

He realizes that the practice is archaic in a time of word processors and VDT units, but finds it a relaxing way to work. "Writing this way," he said, "gives me time to think about what I'm doing. The only problem with this writing method is that materials are hard to find in Memphis."

Picking up a blotter off his desk, he said, "You wouldn't believe how hard it is to find one of these around here."

# Jesse Hill Ford

Jesse Hill Ford showed me around the tiny, cluttered apartment on the Vanderbilt campus that he used as an office. He moved a few boxes and newspapers off the bed. "You can stay here," he said, "and tomorrow we'll take some pictures."

Ford was working on a novel based on Reconstruction and his notes were spread across a door he had propped up on two-by-fours and nailed to the wall. He had rigged up a long florescent lamp across the length of the door and had I not known this was a writer's grotto I would have guessed it was an illegal bookie operation.

Ford, a writer of considerable reputation but not immense popular acclaim, has published four novels, a play, and a collection of short stories. His best-known book, *The Liberation of Lord Byron Jones* (1965), was produced as a movie in 1970. The novel he was at work on is a sequel.

The next day, when Ford returned, we sat in his office and talked. He told me he'd been writing since he was fourteen. He didn't make it a full-time job, however, until 1957, when he quit his job as assistant director of publicity at the American Medical Association in Chicago to move back to Humboldt, Tennessee, to work on a novel. He said he never regretted the move but that it was "a difficult decision quitting a secure job to write books when you had three children to raise."

Coming back to the South was not a hard decision for Ford. Born in Troy, Alabama, he had grown up in Nashville, gone to Vanderbilt, and married the daughter of a Humboldt doctor. "It doesn't offend me to be called a Southern writer," he said when asked about the label. "In fact, it would hurt my feelings if I wasn't called that."

Most of Ford's books are out of print now, a fact that he accepts philosophically. "You always hope that they will come back," he said, fiddling with the tape dispenser on his desk. "What I would really hate," he continued, "would be if I weren't being read, but I am. I was out in Salt Lake City and had to go to two libraries to get a copy of *Liberation* for a lecture. The one I got had been checked out consistently and I was of course pleased about that."

Ford invited me to go fishing at Old Hickory Lake that afternoon. "I think the love of fishing is genetic," he said when I declined the fishing. "Some people are fishermen and some are not."

At the lake he introduced me to his lifelong friend George Cole, who owned the house and the fishing boots and rod Ford was using. After a time I walked down to the lake and yelled to him, "Getting any bites?" "No," he said, "but that doesn't matter. This is like meditation for me. It's what I call being uptown. Downtown is when you're thinking."

# William Price Fox

William Price Fox is one of the funniest, most irreverent, most idiosyncratic writers you'd ever want to meet. He is like a whirlwind, moving in five directions at once, saying yes to everything from garden club speaking engagements to articles for the *Atlantic* and *Golf Digest* and then panicking because he has to be three places on the same day.

Fox is also my friend. He, more than anyone else, is responsible for the five-year journey that resulted in this book. It was Fox who said, after reading my miserable fiction for two years, "Mark, you'd better keep your daytime job. If I were you I'd go back to taking pictures."

The Capital Cafe, a Columbia, South Carolina, institution for years and home base for area good-ole-boys and the politically powerful, seems a perfect background for Fox. Much of his fiction revolves around places like the Capital. Fox says he likes the Capital because it reminds him of his father, who installed the refrigeration units and serviced them.

"My father was a bootlegger, a musician, a chef, and he knew three or four languages even though he didn't finish the fourth grade. When he owned his own restaurant, 'Bill's' on North Main Street, he would get drunk and write out the menus in French. What he'd do was drink vodka out of a coffee cup; he thought he was really fooling everyone. The more he drank the more elegant he became and the more his little finger would go out." Fox said he and his brother and two soldiers got in a fight one night and they all went through a plate glass window. "When we were finished," Fox said, "and were telling Dad what happened, he yelled, 'Get back, dammit! You're getting blood on my menu.'"

Fox said he didn't start out as a writer when he moved to New York City in 1952 to be a salesman. He published his first fiction, disguised as an article in the *Village Voice,* when the regular author made a bet Fox couldn't write the column.

"It was weird," Fox said, "because I never thought about writing, but I did like to read." The article led him to Caroline Gordon's writing class at the New School for Social Research in 1961, and one year later he published a collection of short stories, *Southern Fried,* that has sold three million copies. Since then, he has written three novels, taught at the University of Iowa's Writer's Workshop, written hundreds of articles, and worked in Hollywood as a screenwriter.

Fox, who grew up in Columbia and graduated in medieval history from the University of South Carolina in 1951, came back to his hometown in 1977 to be writer-in-residence. He said his return to the South was much like his return from World War II as a lieutenant.

"I joined the Air Corps when I was sixteen, after I failed the ninth grade," he said, smiling broadly. "When I came back in uniform everybody else in school was about to graduate. They thought I was impersonating an officer and sent the military police after me. When they arrived, I just whipped out my old A.G.O. card and they snapped to attention. They said, 'Sorry sir.' I said, 'That's OK, doggies, at ease.'" Fox laughed. "Nothing has changed. Now they think I'm impersonating a writer-in-residence."

# Ernest J. Gaines

Ernest J. Gaines was sitting at a picnic table in the Baton Rouge, Louisiana, backyard of his friends Betty and Lionel, waiting for Betty to finish cooking collard greens, dressing, and left-over turkey. Gaines had been hard to track down between his San Francisco home and his teaching job at the University of Southwestern Louisiana in Lafayette, an hour's drive from Baton Rouge across the bayou country. Although he was born in rural Louisiana and spent the first fifteen years of his life there, he has lived the last thirty-seven years in California.

Gaines is a Southern writer who still looks across the two thousand miles separating his adopted home and his imaginary home of Bayonne, Louisiana, where all his fiction is set. California, he said, gave him the perspective that made him want to learn more about his native region. "I tried to find books about my own people, and of course they were not available in libraries, even in the San Francisco Bay area. I kept reading, though I didn't find many books about my people. I began to read anything that dealt with the land and with the peasantry and rural life."

"If you're staying inside a house," Gaines said, settling back against the table now, "I don't know if you can see everything that's in there as well as if you went outside and looked in the window."

When he graduated from San Francisco State College in 1957, Gaines said, he gave himself ten years to be a writer. Although he met his deadline for recognition, he has not been able to support himself exclusively on his fiction. "Teaching feeds me and pays the rent and bills because I'm not making it as a writer. Not that I like it. I prefer writing or lying on my boat in San Francisco Bay, but lying on my boat doesn't pay the bills," he said, laughing.

Gaines's biggest commercial success and perhaps his nemesis was *The Autobiography of Miss Jane Pittman,* his third novel, which was made into a successful TV movie starring Cicely Tyson. As is the case with James Dickey, many people recognize Gaines's name only when it is juxtaposed with his most popular work. Gaines said it sometimes bothers him that the public isn't aware of his other books, like *In My Father's House* (1978). "But," he conceded, "I think people usually identify writers with certain books, like Tolstoy and *War and Peace,* and forget the rest."

"I told my sister recently," he said, laughing, "that if I died tomorrow they could bury me, but don't put anything about *Miss Jane* on my tombstone. Put anything else you want, but not that."

Betty sent Lionel out to tell us that lunch was ready. As we walked to the house I asked Gaines if he ever ran across any students as ambitious as he had been. Oh yes, he said. "You can run across what you consider talent. However, in the beginning we all seem to have talent. It takes work. Writing is a discipline, and you have to keep sitting at the desk by yourself and write and write and write and write."

# George Garrett

George Garrett is a writer who changes addresses as nonchalantly as most people change their clothes.

Garrett was in Columbia, South Carolina, a town he has also called home, to visit his friend the novelist Ben Greer. At the time, he was between teaching jobs and working on his novel *The Succession,* which was published in 1983.

"Not counting the crosstown moves," Garrett told Greer and me while sitting in a local bar, "we've moved into fifteen different places in the last twenty years. My wife told me the last move was it and if I go again, I go alone." He laughed and spun his cap around on his hand.

If any writer could be called garrulous, Garrett certainly is a candidate. He is known as much for his personality and his willingness to help others as he is for his own work. "It seems to me a teacher has a certain kind of obligation to try and help people," Garrett said. "But you must remember that any advice an artist might give you could be dead wrong, so it's not so much a question of advice, but support. It gives an artist the sense that he is not completely alone."

Garrett said he had very little help when he started his writing career except for the support of his family. Nonetheless, he has published twenty books and written scripts for five movies since his first book of poems was published in 1957. But even with his impressive list of published works, Garrett has always had to teach to support himself. "Obviously, it would be better not to teach," he said, "but I don't know many writers for whom that's true. I probably thought every year this was going to be temporary, but it's getting close to thirty years now."

Between rounds of scotch and water, Greer asked Garrett about the time, long ago, when he was a boxer. "It's true," he said to us, "I did box and got pretty good at it. I've always been kind of cocky because I didn't have all those marks on my face, but a dentist told me recently that every one of my teeth is shattered. Another doctor looked at my nose and said, 'Boy, somebody's been beating your nose with a hammer.'" Garrett laughed, drawing much attention from the other bar patrons.

Greer told Garrett he'd been contacted that week about writing a screenplay. Garrett snapped his fingers and grabbed Greer's arm. "You know, one of my films, *Frankenstein Meets the Space Monster,* won a Golden Turkey Award," he said, laughing.

"I guess you're real proud of that?" Greer said.

"I just sort of ignored it for a long time," Garrett said, "but then I began to get proud of it being one of the worst one hundred films of all time. You know," he said, leaning back in his chair, "it's the only film I know that is greatly improved by continual commercial interruption. It's also the only film I've ever seen at a drive-in where people blew their horns to get it off the screen."

# Ellen Gilchrist

The phone rang, interrupting the funny story Ellen Gilchrist was telling as she curled up on the bed at her mother's home in Jackson, Mississippi. It was a friend who had read her new book of short stories, *Victory Over Japan*. "You read it?" Gilchrist said effusively. "You do? . . . I'm so glad."

She was still excited about the reviews she had gotten the week before in the *New York Times* and the *Washington Post*. "If I'm ever going to be famous," she said, "this is as good as it gets." *Victory Over Japan* won the 1984 American Book Award a few months later.

Gilchrist is a very funny, sometimes irreverent woman. I was afraid all our pictures would be of a woman rolled over on her side laughing. I told her that I was going to New Orleans to visit friends. "Oh, don't do that," she said, even though she lived there fourteen years.

"Well, people from Mississippi sort of naturally hate New Orleans," she explained. "They go down there and New Orleans eats them alive. They can't get into the Boston Club unless they stay there for twenty years and are real obedient," she said laughing. "We all grew up listening to New Orleans radio stations in the middle of the night, but we're all still prettier and smarter than they are, but they won't admit it."

Although she looked to be a woman in her thirties, Gilchrist is, in fact, a mother of three and a grandmother of two. She was born in Vicksburg, Mississippi, and grew up in Jackson where she was a student of Eudora Welty the only year Welty ever taught at Millsaps College.

Gilchrist's mother, a young-looking seventy, made an energetic entrance as if cued from offstage. She told Gilchrist she had run into someone when she was in town who "just loved every minute of your new book."

"We need some music," Gilchrist told her mother mischievously. "Will you bring me a radio in here and put it on some top forty. Get in here and wait on me. I'm being made famous."

When she was forty-four, Gilchrist said, she ran her first marathon. That same year she published *In the Land of Dreamy Dreams,* her first book of short stories. "But," she said, "I'd been writing all my life. I had a newspaper column when I was thirteen and had my picture in the paper every week."

Gilchrist had come to Jackson from her home in Fayetteville, Arkansas. She was leaving for New York City, where she planned to spend three months working on a new novel. But she said her plans had gone awry. "I had such great plans for New York," she said, laughing, "but instead I've invited everybody I know to come visit me. If they all come, it will just be a big three-month-long party."

# Gail Godwin

Against my better judgment, I had given Gail Godwin my camera and she was leaning back on the bed at the Marriott in Columbia, South Carolina, taking pictures of me on the sofa. "That's right, put your feet there. Now, move your head to the left. Perfect. Great," she said, mimicking photographers. "I just like to know how the other person feels," she said after exhausting the last roll of film.

Godwin, who worked for two years at the *Miami Herald* after graduating from the University of North Carolina in 1959, had no trouble assuming the role. "But," she said, "I always wanted to write fiction. Journalism was a practical decision. I thought I'd better train in something that would pay a salary."

Eventually, fiction got her into trouble at the *Herald*. "I made a couple of factual errors and they had to run a retraction," she said, "so I'm better off in fiction." She was reluctantly fired from the *Herald* and worked from 1962 to 1965 with the U.S. Travel Service in London. When she returned to the United States in 1967 to get her master's at the University of Iowa, Godwin said, she had already learned more than she realized.

"London is where I really got my education," she said. "I read all the novels I'd never read before. I wrote a novel. It was a perfect job for someone in her early twenties who wanted to write but needed money and experience."

Her experience in Europe and her second failed marriage there resulted in her first novel, *The Perfectionists* (1970). The following year she got her Ph.D. from Iowa, where her fellow classmates included John Irving, John Casey, and Jane Barnes and one of her teachers was Kurt Vonnegut. "There was a hotspot of energy when I was there," Godwin said. "We were all reading each other's work and in competition with each other."

The final galley of Godwin's new book, *The Finishing School,* was lying on the coffee table. Recalling that her most popular book, *A Mother and Two Daughters,* had been nominated for the National Book Award in 1982 and had been on the *New York Times* best-seller list for most of that year, I asked her if she ever got tired of interviews. "Some I enjoy," she said, "but *People* magazine came for a total of eleven hours, counting the photographer's separate trip, and I had to let them. By the time it was over I was exhausted. I saw stacks and stacks of proofs, and you just get sick of looking at your face after a while."

Godwin, who lives in Woodstock, New York, with composer Robert Starer, said the "autobiographical fiction" questions bother her the most. "If anyone else asks me if my fiction is autobiographical. . . .What does that mean?" she said. "Sometimes, someone asks me a question that makes me think and I'm very glad when that happens."

# Paul Green

Paul Green was standing on the front porch of his white farmhouse surveying the peaceful North Carolina countryside when I drove my car up the gravel road. He raised a hand, signaling me to come through the gate, which was counter-balanced by a cannonball.

"Beautiful, isn't it?" he said as I stepped on the porch. "But it's February and still a little early to be standing out here, I guess."

Green, who was eighty-six years old at the time of our meeting, was a tall man with a straight back and large hands that seemed to get in the way occasionally. He walked to the door, his hands swallowing the tiny doorknob, and invited me inside. Green's home seemed to be all books, music, and light. Large windows lit every corner, and a piano with stacks of music dominated the center of the room. Even his book-lined study appeared to be roofless, like a set from one of his outdoor dramas.

At the back of the house a picture window let in the soft light of a cloudy winter morning. I walked to the window, marveling at the stark beauty of the countryside. Green followed and stood behind me. "You should see it in the spring," he said, naming all the trees and plants that would soon be budding and blooming.

Green, who was born in 1894 in Lillington, North Carolina, and who won a Pulitzer Prize in 1927 for his play *In Abraham's Bosom,* was a re-markable man, not only for the state of his health but also for his intelligence. He knew Aristotle and Kant as well as he knew the growing season for summer squash. He was also a man of vision who had a lifelong history of attacking prejudice and ignorance.

"I have always felt," he said, "that racism and prejudice in any form are wrong." He recalled how some residents of Chapel Hill reacted to the sight of writer Richard Wright riding between his Carr-boro boardinghouse and Green's house with Green's secretary as driver. Green had heard ru-mors of violence and, as he recalled, "I went out to the boardinghouse and stood guard all night in the field next to Wright's house just in case any-one wanted to cause trouble. It was sad to see such a great writer treated that way."

Elizabeth, Green's wife of sixty years, inter-rupted our conversation and said lunch was ready. It was an honest country meal of boiled potatoes, green beans, and homemade bread. Green talked about the garden he was getting ready to plant and apologized for last year's canned vegetables. "You come back here to see us this summer," he said, "and we'll give you some fresh vegetables for dinner. I tell you, nothing is better."

Green liked the photographs I sent him later. "They strike me as right," he wrote, "the pho-tographed witness of much in this world and of a struggler (fighter even) in the cause."

Green died a few weeks later, on May 4, 1981.

# Barry Hannah

Barry Hannah was sitting on the front porch of his Oxford, Mississippi, home, feet propped up against a support and balancing on the back legs of a kitchen chair, when the phone rang. "Damn," he said, as he righted himself and lost his spot in the afternoon sun.

He was gone only a few minutes before a resounding "Ye-ha!" shattered the peaceful Mississippi springtime. Hannah flung open the screen door and raised two clinched fists like a boxer claiming victory. "My agent sold my book," he said as he walked across the yard to tell his neighbors.

Hannah, like Harry Crews, has a reputation as a hard-drinking, hard-living man. A tough guy. He had been in his native Mississippi only a few months after teaching at Iowa's Writer's Workshop and writing scripts for Robert Altman in Hollywood, but already the slow life-style seemed to have had a calming effect. He said he was a much happier person since coming back to Ole Miss to teach.

"I just find a lot of pleasure and love in my good friends here like Willie Morris," he said, settling back into his chair. "But, you know, the fact of the matter is that life is boring sometimes and there are a number of things you have to do and if you don't have interesting friends it's kind of a dusty trip." Hannah smiled. "I mean, if you're not drinking or you're not reading an interesting book, or in direct pursuit of a woman, it's really a slow trip."

Hannah, who was born and grew up in Clinton, Mississippi, is known for his funny, incisive, and original books. *Geronimo Rex,* published in 1972, was called a brilliant first novel by most critics and was nominated for a National Book Award. Hannah's fifth book, *The Tennis Handsome* (1983), is a collection of his comic prose including the famous story "Midnight and I'm Not Famous Yet," which first appeared in *Airships* (1978) and which singer Jimmy Buffet made into one of his more memorable songs.

Hannah is just as funny and off-center as his stories. He is a natural storyteller and able to tell you almost anything with a straight face. When an attractive coed stopped to watch our photo session on the campus, he told her I was with *Life* magazine and that we could make her famous. Impressed, she agreed to sit next to him long enough for him to get a phone number. He laughed and tore up the number when she left. "I just made her day," he said. "I'll tell her the truth if I ever see her again."

Later, over beers at a local college hangout where we were served by Faulkner's stepdaughter's granddaughter (people in Oxford go to great lengths to trace their lineage to Faulkner), I asked Hannah jokingly what he planned to do with his life now that he was a famous novelist with five books under his belt. He thought a minute, took a sip of beer, and said with great sincerity, "The point of life is to make love to beautiful women, have children, to have fun with nature without abusing it, and to die an honorable death."

# Elizabeth Hardwick

Elizabeth Hardwick left her native Kentucky for New York City at the age of twenty-three after receiving both her B.A. and M.A. from the University of Kentucky.

She has lived in many places, including Europe and the Midwest, but has never returned to live in her native South. "I am very much 'from' Kentucky as a person," Hardwick told me, "and it is very much here and there in my writing. I think having grown up in the South has been of great value—the sense of knowing the place or having known it for important years. The people, the landscape, my family, my education, of course all that remains."

Hardwick came to New York to study literature at Columbia University. She says she hasn't cultivated a Southern image and that her later work has "taken its frame from the intellectual and creative life in New York. Kentucky," she says, "and especially Lexington, is a beautiful place, but I am not drawn to racing and farming as a source and so can't claim a true attachment for the Bluegrass passion."

Hardwick's first novel, *The Ghostly Lover* (1945), is set in the South and New York, and her last, *Sleepless Nights* (1979), concerns a woman looking back to her Kentucky beginnings. In between those two novels, Hardwick married poet Robert Lowell, was awarded a Guggenheim Fellowship, and established herself as one of America's premier essayists, short story writers, and novelists. She was also one of the founders of the *New York Review of Books* in 1963, along with Lowell, Robert Silvers, and Jason and Barbara Epstein.

Although she has lived away from the South for many years, Hardwick still speaks with a pleasant and sophisticated Southern accent. She is a friendly, open woman with a wry sense of humor. I asked her if she ever felt her marriage to Lowell overshadowed her own career.

"Well, I should hope so," she said smiling. "I consider Robert Lowell a writer of almost incredible talent and achievement and it was a great privilege for me to be in the presence of a mind so fine and a dedication to literature so complete. I am sure whatever talent I have was greatly increased by my marriage."

# Beth Henley

A guard opened the stage door of St. Michael's Theatre on Forty-ninth Street in New York City and pointed down a dark hallway. "I think she's down there," he said. The steady beat of rock music echoed off the high ceiling and a flight of steps led down to the source. Beth Henley, barely thirty and already a Pulitzer Prize-winning playwright, was on the floor in tights and legwarmers in the middle of an aerobic workout.

Upstairs, Henley's new play, *The Wake of Jamie Foster,* was in rehearsal and the workout was Henley's lunch break. She jogged over after the music stopped, introduced herself, and asked if I could wait around an hour while she did an interview with the *New York Times.*

Henley was born in Jackson, Mississippi, the daughter of a Mississippi state senator. Although she was vaguely interested in writing while in high school, she didn't take any play-writing classes until her sophomore year at Southern Methodist University in Dallas. But Henley did not see herself as a playwright, even after a year of graduate school at the University of Illinois. "I started out as an actor," she told me when she returned from the *Times* interview, "and I only wrote plays because I couldn't get any serious work as an actor." Henley left school and moved to Los Angeles in 1976. Over the next three years she had mostly temporary jobs and "never got any good acting jobs," she said. She wrote her prizewinning play *Crimes of the Heart* in 1978 and reworked it many times before it was produced at the Louisville, Kentucky, play-writing competition the following year.

Now it was three years later, the Broadway premiere of her second play was only weeks away, and she was in the middle of major revisions. She did not seem worried and was genuinely unassuming about the attention being heaped on her. "I guess you want me up here," she said with a laugh as she hopped up on a wobbly table that was part of the stage furniture. It was obvious that she had had some experience acting. The camera did not make her shy or uncomfortable, and the conversation was more like visiting a college friend.

Henley's director sent an assistant down to check on his playwright. Then the stage manager walked on the set and said he needed the second stage for other rehearsals. "I'm sorry," Henley said in her still-unaffected Mississippi accent, "but I've got to get back to work, too."

I asked her what her plans were, wondering whether she might return to the South, but she said she planned to stay in Los Angeles for now because "I like eating Mexican food and being anonymous and living near the ocean."

# Madison Jones

"Oh me," Madison Jones said in his slow, precise Tennessee drawl when I told him of a friend who had quit his job to write a novel. He shook his head, kneading fistfuls of skin hanging down from the neck of his favorite dog. "That's a mighty dangerous thing to do," he said, leaning over in his chair and continuing to pet Doc. "There's an awful disproportion between the number of writers and the number of readers. All chiefs and no Indians," he said, laughing.

Jones has been writer-in-residence at Auburn University in Alabama since he published his first novel, *The Innocent,* in 1957. His devastating deadpan humor is genuine, but there is also a sadness in the man Flannery O'Connor admired and mentioned a dozen times in her letters.

"She tried to help me out," Jones said. "She wrote me about my first novel and we became friends." He said O'Connor even gave him a few geese and ducks, but the descendants don't roam Shiloh, his farm near Auburn. "I went out of town once," he said matter-of-factly, "and some kids were to look after them. They didn't, of course, and the ducks and geese all starved to death while I was gone."

Jones said that although he is not sorry he became a writer, he had "been a good deal discouraged in the past couple of years." Most of his books are out of print, including his 1971 novel *A Cry of Absence,* which poet Allen Tate called "a masterpiece of fictional art." "When people ask me the advice I would give a young writer," Jones said, not letting on the humorous nature of his response, "I tell them to stop before it's too late."

Jones does think that too many writers are being encouraged too much. "I think a lot of people are wasting an awful lot of time," he said, taking a puff from his cigar and smiling broadly. "Writing conferences and programs are supposed to produce greater amounts of creative effort, which in turn is supposed to create more good books, but I doubt if it does."

Jones's career has not been all bad luck. Hollywood found him in 1967 and made a movie of his novel *An Exile.* The film, retitled *I Walk the Line,* starred Gregory Peck and Tuesday Weld with Johnny Cash providing the soundtrack music.

As we were walking around the Auburn campus, I spotted a student reading a historical romance. "You think you could ever write a novel like that just for money?" I asked him.

Jones smiled, but I could see he was considering the question seriously. "I've thought about it a whole lot from time to time," he said. "I've thought, I'll just give it a whirl, but I don't think I'm capable of writing that kind of book. It just wouldn't hold my interest." Then he added, "Writers who write those kinds of books have a kind of talent, too. They are just writers with a cheap talent."

# Donald Justice

Donald Justice is a poet John Irving described in his 1981 novel *The Hotel New Hampshire* as "a man you'd ask to say an elegy for someone you'd loved." Irving, who knew Justice when they were both teaching at Iowa ten years earlier, quoted a number of Justice's poems in the novel. "I'd like to think that my poems sold a lot of books for John," Justice told me, laughing.

When I photographed him in 1981, he was taking a year-long break from the harsh winters of Iowa as visiting professor at the University of Virginia in Charlottesville. Although he was living among the possessions of others, the home and furnishings seemed to suit the personality of the poet. When we came upon a baby grand piano in the study, Justice told me that he had thought about being a musician and had studied composition under Carl Ruggles. He sat down and on request played the slow movement of a Mozart sonata.

"I wanted to be a composer throughout adolescence and into college," Justice said when he had finished the piece, "but I decided at some point that I wasn't good enough and gave it up."

"And then you went into something really profitable like poetry," I said. "Well, not exactly," he said, laughing. "I teach to make a living, like most poets have done for at least a generation."

Even though he grew up in Miami, and taught at the University of Iowa for twenty years before moving to the University of Florida at Gainesville recently, Justice still sometimes thinks of himself as a Southern writer. "Miami wouldn't be considered a Southern city now," he said, "but it certainly was in the old days in the neighborhood I grew up in. Everybody was from Georgia or Alabama or South Carolina. The sheriffs were all from Georgia. If somebody was from, say, North Carolina, it was like being from another country."

Justice played a dissonant chord on the baby grand when I asked him the obvious question. "No," he said, "I don't think there is any connection between my poetry and music. It seems to me that poetry, literature, and music come from a similar way of feeling about the world and there's no more specific connection."

Justice, who won the 1980 Pulitzer Prize for poetry, speaks in precise, measured sentences like his poetry. He said he thought the writers of his generation were happier than the previous one. "But," he said, "my guess is that the happiest artists are painters. Renoir, from what I've read, was a man whose life was full of joy. I suppose writers are the second happiest."

Are writers who are read happier than those who are not? I asked. Justice thought for a moment. "Why not? I never felt it was right for the thing I write out of love just to lie around, unnoticed," he said. "I want it to get around. The first pleasure, yes, is the pleasure of creation, but then there is that second pleasure."

# John Oliver Killens

New York is a long way from Macon, Georgia, and it was even farther, at least in racial attitude, when John Oliver Killens left his union-organizing job and moved to Brooklyn in 1948 to be a writer. It was not Killens's first trip to New York or his first attempt at writing. He had been writing since the eighth grade, and even started a novel once. "I got forty pages into it and gave up," he told me, sitting in his study in Brooklyn. "I just got disgusted with myself, but, you see, I hadn't lived long enough to write a novel."

When Killens was drafted into the army from law school during World War II, he used writing as an escape during respites from the combat zone. "The writing bug bit me again out there in the South Pacific," he said, "and a few years after I got home I heard about a workshop at Columbia University and I sent them a manuscript because at the time I needed someone to tell me I wasn't wasting my time writing."

The workshop's response to his work told him he wasn't wasting his time, and when he read the first chapter of his controversial 1954 novel *Youngblood* to the Harlem Writers Guild, which he co-founded along with three others, the response was enthusiastic but troubled. "They told me, this is great stuff, John, but ain't nobody going to publish it."

Killens hardly seems like an activist. He is a soft-spoken and articulate man who chooses his words carefully. His home on Union Street is practically a museum of original works by black American and African artists. Killens said he is intensely proud of his heritage, both as a black man and as a Southerner. He still travels to Macon occasionally to see old high school friends and "kinda keep my hand in."

"I write as a black man from Georgia," Killens told me, explaining his Southern perspective, "in a time of a very racist society, and it's from that perspective that I see the world around me." He said he's tried to instill his pride, both as a black man and as a writer, in his students at Medgar Evers College in Brooklyn where he is writer-in-residence. "Writers," he said, "should write with integrity and without the tastes of the publishers or public in mind."

But isn't that a formula for failure—at least, commercial failure? I asked him. "You have to have confidence to be a writer," Killens said. "People say to me, 'John, how can you sit upstairs and type on a book thinking you have something so important to say instead of getting out here in the struggle?' I always answer that a writer has to reconcile the contradiction of the absolute need for solitude versus the equally absolute need for experience with other human beings, since he or she cannot suck experiences out of a thumb. Hence the need to be a writer-activist."

# Andrew Lytle

Andrew Lytle's cabin in Monteagle, Tennessee, was his mother's summerhouse. It was also Lytle's home when he married Edna Barker in 1938. "I married during the Depression," Lytle told me, "and the place was run-down. Snow drifted in. I worked here and we cooked on the hearth. It was so cold that a bucket of water froze in front of the fireplace going full blast. My father said, 'If she'll live with you through that, then she'll live with you.'"

Lytle laughed. It was hard to tell if the frozen water had been an apocryphal addition, but it didn't seem to matter. Great storytellers always leave a little doubt at the end of their tales.

Lytle, of course, is interesting with or without the stories. After graduating in 1918 from nearby Sewanee Military Academy at sixteen, he sailed for France, and a year later for England. Although he planned to attend Exeter College, Oxford, he returned to Vanderbilt when he learned his grandfather was ill. The return in 1921 was fateful. Lytle became friends with a young writer named Robert Penn Warren who was a member of a group called the Fugitives, along with Allen Tate, John Crowe Ransom, and Donald Davidson. Although Lytle never joined the Fugitives, he eventually contributed an essay to the famous Agrarian symposium *I'll Take My Stand.*

In 1927 Lytle went to New York, where he earned his living as an actor. In his spare time he went to the New York Public Library and read books on the Civil War. He became so interested in the subject that he decided to write a book which he completed in his hometown of Murfreesboro, Tennessee, in 1930.

After publishing *Bedford Forrest and His Critter Company* (1931), Lytle moved to his father's farm near Guntersville, Alabama, to begin work on his first novel, *The Long Night.* "Behind the house was a hill," Lytle said, "and I would go up there, put a board across my lap, and work all day. The birds and the animals all took me for granted. In the evening when I returned my father would ask me how the muse had treated me that day."

Lytle published four novels between 1936 and 1957. He also taught Flannery O'Connor at the University of Iowa in 1946 and 1947 and started the writing program at the University of Florida in Gainesville.

Lytle still writes every day and likes to travel. When he lectures he can always be found at parties surrounding an author's arrival, drinking his special bourbon from a silver cup. "It tastes better out of silver," Lytle told me. "The cups don't break and it has some ritual to it. I tell anyone who asks that anything but silver mortifies my lips."

Lytle said his writing now is confined to critical essays in journals like the *Sewanee Review,* which he edited for fifteen years. "Do you think you'll ever write another novel?" I asked him.

"I don't think I can write any more fiction," Lytle said, picking up his silver cup. "It's too hard and I don't have anything more to say."

# Cormac McCarthy

Cormac McCarthy was hard to track down. No one seemed to know where he lived. An editor said New Mexico, another writer said Europe, and the library reference book said New York.

They were all wrong. McCarthy was living in a 10 × 10-foot motel room in Knoxville, Tennessee, with a portable typewriter, stacks of books, and authentic motel furniture. It had taken several months for a letter to go through his publisher's office and through several forwarding procedures to finally end up at the Colonial Motel on Kingston Street.

McCarthy grew up in Knoxville, the setting of two of his novels, and said he had returned home via Arizona, Mexico, Texas, and Santa Fe, New Mexico, to finish his new book, which he described as a Southwestern novel. "I just decide to go to a place," he said, "take a room, and write."

McCarthy has had this nomadic life-style since *The Orchard Keeper* won the 1965 Faulkner Foundation Award for best first novel. He received an American Academy of Arts and Letters grant before his first novel was even published, and left for Europe instead of doing interviews and promotional tours. "Selling a book is the job of the publisher," he said. "Besides, Random House has enough sense to know that they're not going to sell many of my books no matter what they do. They just like to have a few people on their list who can construct a sentence."

After his 1965 grant ran out, a Rockefeller Foundation grant gave him two more years in London and Paris and on the island of Ibiza in the Balearics while he finished his second novel, *Outer Dark,* published in 1968. Other grants followed, including two Guggenheim Fellowships and in 1982 a grant from the MacArthur Foundation, which pays an artist up to sixty thousand tax-free dollars a year for five years.

Through all the grants and critical praise for his complex novels, McCarthy maintains a quirky sense of humor about his art. "If your ego is so inverted that you really think the world wants to hear about what you did and thought," he said, smiling, "then there's something very much wrong with you. It's an extraordinary point of view to take."

It was obvious we couldn't take the picture in his motel room. McCarthy suggested a tour of the city in his '64 Rambler. He put a Wagner opera in the tape player and turned up the volume. For some reason, we ended up at the old Knoxville train station. The building, which later became an expensive restaurant, was empty except for the refuse of Knoxville's street people. The setting seemed perfect for someone like McCarthy. He got behind a ticket booth and pretended to call out stops down the line. "This is the window where you get a ticket with the destination left blank," he said, laughing.

Driving back to the motel I asked him if it ever bothered him that other writers were famous and he was not. "One of the great hurdles of life," he said, turning down the aria, "is when you can forget about what other people are doing."

# David Madden

The choice of library as background for David Madden's photograph was an obvious one. Madden's rambling circa 1912 home in Baton Rouge, Louisiana, is a virtual public library, with more volumes lining the walls than most small-town library collections. It is hard to imagine having a collection of books as large as his without evoking Dewey Decimal to aid in finding individual volumes, but Madden seemed to know the exact location of every book.

"I have a very interesting collection of a thousand paperbacks up here," he told me, pointing the way to an upstairs room lined with books. There he showed me a 1940s Penguin edition of Erskine Caldwell's *God's Little Acre* with the famous Jonas "knot-hole" cover and a paperback of Thomas Wolfe's short stories that, he told me, "I stole from a drugstore in Knoxville when I was thirteen. I even used it in a lecture on Wolfe recently."

Madden, who admits to being slightly reclusive, is a prolific writer of fiction, poetry, drama, and criticism. His enormous old L&N Railroad desk sometimes has five different books in progress at various locations across the top.

The day I visited Madden he was working on a Civil War novel called *Sharpshooter* which is set in his native Knoxville. Around the walls of his study were pictures of Civil War heroes—Stonewall Jackson, Nathan Bedford Forrest, and Ulysses S. Grant. Sharing the wall space with Civil War heroes were Madden's literary heroes—William Faulkner, James Joyce, Thomas Wolfe, and Wright Morris.

But Madden has not spent his entire life insulated from the world by his books. He quit college after his freshman year to become a New York City mail clerk. Then he joined the merchant marines and sailed the world, eventually enlisting as an army private in the early 1950s.

Madden thinks these past adventures and an optimistic attitude keep him from being what he laughingly called "an effete snob." "I don't have sports interests. I don't fish, I don't gamble, and I don't drink or smoke," he said, explaining his independent nature. "I also don't pal around with writers because that requires drinking. I just don't see why writers think that drinking and smoking a lot is interesting to write or talk about."

Although he has been writer-in-residence at Louisiana State University since 1968, Madden's main source of income is still writing. He pointed out a shelf with copies of *Bijou* (1974) and *Pleasure Dome* (1979) alongside his five other novels, his two collections of stories, and a few volumes of his critical essays. "With all that, I should be as rich and famous as Norman Mailer," he said laughing, "but I'm not. So what else is new?"

# Marion Montgomery

Marion Montgomery was sitting on the porch of his Crawford, Georgia, home looking very much like a gentleman farmer in his Sunday-go-to-meeting suit and newly polished Georgia Giants boots. "My wife thought I should dress up for this picture," he said with a smile, getting out of his rocker and extending a hand.

Montgomery is a genuine Southern writer if anybody can be given that label. Except for two years at the University of Iowa's Writers Workshop, he has spent his entire life in Georgia. He got his undergraduate and graduate degrees from the University of Georgia in Athens and has taught there for over thirty years.

Although he has written fifteen books, published fiction and poetry in dozens of magazines and journals, and had his work anthologized in several important short story collections, Montgomery's work remains largely unknown. "I'm always surprised at somebody who knows my work," he said in his slow, precise Georgia drawl. "I suppose fame would be a kind of pleasure, but I certainly don't brood on the fact that I'm not likely to encounter anybody reading my books on a bus." Montgomery laughed.

"So you agree with Yeats," I asked, "that an artist should learn to exult in his work without public adulation?"

"I would put it another way," he said. "You just have to do what you can do and accept it. You don't have time to exult over it. You leave that to others. If your work is any good, it won't be lost."

Montgomery has written three novels and two collections of poems since his first book of poems, *Dry Lightning,* was published in 1960. His last novel, *Fugitive,* was published in 1974. He said work on a critical trilogy has "taken up the last ten or fifteen years," but that he plans to write another novel, even though the market is glutted these days. "I suspect I would have less trouble getting a good reading," he said, "but I don't envy the person who has his first novel ready to be read."

Montgomery's wife walked out on the porch and cast a suspicious eye at his boots. "They're real comfortable shoes," Montgomery said, taking a puff off his cigar and explaining his reasons for wearing them to no one in particular. "I had expected to wear them to my oldest daughter's wedding and at the last minute they persuaded me not to. My youngest daughter says she won't get married if I *don't* wear them."

# Guy Owen

Guy Owen seemed to be the lone inhabitant of the North Carolina State University campus when I found him in the English department in September of 1979. Owen's office was at the end of a long hall. He was so involved in his work that not even the sound of footsteps reverberating off the high ceiling made him look over the stacks of papers and books and out his open door. I knocked timidly and Owen looked up, surprised at first to see me, but then he smiled and extended his hand.

"Sorry, I didn't hear you come in," he said, "but I've got to finish editing this book before classes start. Once they start, I've got to pretty much close up shop until Christmas and summer."

At the time, I hadn't begun to photograph writers. I wasn't even sure who wore the label "Southern writer," and I was counting on Owen to counsel me on the subject. He suggested we go to a nearby diner for lunch, and when the waiter brought our coffee Owen took a sip and said mischievously, "So you want to photograph Southern writers? Well, my friend, I'm afraid you'll find that a very low-paying endeavor." He laughed and took off his glasses, cleaning them with his coffee-stained napkin.

Owen knew most writers of merit and had published some of the best in the *Southern Poetry Review*, which he founded and edited until 1975. He was very enthusiastic about my book and suggested twenty-five or so names before he noticed that I was writing the names on a napkin. "I'll give you a list back at the office," he said, smiling.

As we walked back through the campus he talked about his work. He had been publishing books since 1960 (*Season of Fear*) and was nominated for the 1970 Pulitzer Prize for *Journey for Joedel*. His most famous book, *The Ballad of the Flim-Flam Man* (1965), had been made into a popular movie. But in 1979 Owen was having trouble finding a publisher for his fifth novel, and I could see the lack of success was painful. "It's harder than ever to publish these days," he said, "even if you've been published before."

Owen was not, however, a writer who dwelled on failure, and the sight of an operating sprinkler system reminded him of a story about a man looking for water with a divining rod. He was a great storyteller and laughed at the punchline until he had to wipe tears from his eyes.

Back at his office he gave me a list of writers he thought I should consider. I had taken a few photographs on our walk and clicked off a few more with Owen's office as background. I told him we would take more photographs later when I had generated some interest in the project. He encouraged me to continue with the book, but warned, "I wouldn't take this too far without a contract." That turned out to be the only advice of his I ignored.

During the next year and a half Owen and I met several times, but never in Raleigh. He would always laugh and say, "Just drop by any time you're up my way and take some more pictures." Unfortunately we put the second session off too long. Guy died in the spring of 1981.

# Walker Percy

The first letter I got from Walker Percy—a note scribbled on a postcard—was not encouraging. Although it was difficult to decipher the hieroglyphic scrawl, the message was "Forget it."

"Thanks, Mark," he wrote, "but I finally had to swear off getting my picture took. To feel foreign for several hours! Jill Krementz wanted three days. Thanks anyway, Walker Percy."

I wrote back immediately. "Alright. Two hours is a long time. Give me ten minutes. You won't even know I've been there. Just one picture is all I'm asking. That's better than Jill K."

Percy wrote back in a few weeks. "OK, you've got an hour," he said, and told me to meet him at Bechac's Restaurant on Lake Pontchartrain, a twenty-minute drive from his home in Covington, Louisiana. I had never seen him before, but when an entourage of men and women filed into Bechac's three weeks later, I knew the tall, lean, white-haired leader must be Walker Percy.

Percy is a writer who is hard to label. All his novels from the first, *The Moviegoer,* which won the 1965 National Book Award, to his latest, *The Second Coming* (1981), are set in the South. The protagonist is always descended from an established Southern family and is generally well-heeled. After that, Percy's novels are hard to label Southern.

Percy led his troop over to my table and introduced his friends: an artist, a journalist, and an assortment of writers and poets who met regularly to discuss their work. The conversation was as mixed a bag as the Louisiana gumbo the waiters put down in front of each of us. After lunch I followed Percy's little blue truck to Covington, the town where he's called Dr. Percy by many of the residents. Percy did finish Columbia University's medical school in 1941, but during his internship contracted tuberculosis and because of his health never practiced. "They just think I'm a doctor who writes magazine articles," he said, smiling.

Percy liked the pictures we took that day more than I did and as a result of the photographs we became friends. When my birthday approached last year, I called him to see if I could "turn thirty with my favorite writer." We spent most of the day talking about books and writers and even talked about his new book, *Lost in the Cosmos* (1983). After taking pictures on the porch of his new Cajun cottage, a three-room dwelling backed up to the Louisiana bayou, I asked him if he had any advice for someone turning thirty.

"I'll tell you something," Percy said, shaking his head, "the day I turned thirty was one of the worst days of my life. I really thought my life was a complete waste. I just thought I was never going to amount to anything."

# Reynolds Price

Reynolds Price is a writer who feels a great attachment to the land and people of his fiction. Although he has traveled extensively, first as a Rhodes Scholar at Merton College, Oxford, Price has always returned to the hills of his native North Carolina. "It's part of the condition of being rooted," he told me. "You're rooted if you can get away. I don't know what would have happened if I'd been strapped to the floor here."

It was Eudora Welty who first saw the "sense of place" in Price's stories when she visited Duke University in 1955. "She singled out my story 'Thomas Egerton,' and her praise encouraged me greatly," Price said. "There's a bond between us in our lives and in our work, but it was not something I was very conscious of in the beginning."

When he returned to Duke in 1958 to teach English after three years in England, he began *A Long and Happy Life,* the novel which won the Faulkner Foundation Award in 1962. Since then, he has written eleven other books and except for a few interruptions to take temporary teaching posts at other universities, he has remained at Duke.

Price said he has taught many good writers over the years, but that "it was beginner's luck to say the least" when Anne Tyler walked up to his table on registration day to sign up as the first student of his first class. "I was twenty-five and she was sixteen, and we both thought this was going to be the way it would be from then on," he said, laughing.

Price said he has taught several exceptionally talented writers in the last few years and feels "vindicated" by the Southern renascence. "Only nine years ago, when *The Surface of the Earth* was published, there was the famous front-page review in the *Times* that claimed Southern fiction had been dead for decades. It's very amusing to me to see a whole new wave of Southern writers in their twenties and thirties who are writing fiction that doesn't mimic the themes and situations of classic Southern fiction but that is still recognizably Southern."

Price said he thinks the new wave of Southern fiction is a result of the sixties generation taking longer to get started, "for various social and personal reasons. That's fine," he said. "Why should writers publish in their twenties? People live longer now."

He picked up a string of worry beads and began to run them through his fingers. I noticed the statue of Krishna kicking the ball of life around the eternal circle and asked him if he was interested in Eastern religions. He smiled. "I am a religious person," he said, "and I consider myself a Christian, but I'm not a Hari Krishna. I just happened to buy that statue in New York when I saw it in a window of a store going out of business."

He put down the beads and smiled. "I'm eastern North Carolina, but that's all."

# Larry Rubin

A few Southern writers are not typical Southerners. They are what poet Larry Rubin calls "transplanted Yankees." Rubin came to the South—Miami, Florida—from Bayonne, New Jersey, when he was a child, moved to Atlanta, and left only to spend four years in Poland, Norway, Germany, and Austria as a Fulbright Scholar.

"I came to the real South when I was seventeen to attend Emory University," Rubin said, "and I've been here ever since." Now, at fifty-five, Rubin says he considers himself "an absolute Southerner." He says Southern journals are the most receptive markets for his poems, although "I like to think of my poetry as very cosmopolitan."

Rubin has been teaching English at Georgia Tech in Atlanta since 1955. I asked him if he ever convinces any prospective engineers that they should go into liberal arts. "Believe it or not," he said, putting his hands in his rumpled coat pockets, "I do. And some want to write poetry. It's rather rare. Our greatest triumph is when we get one to go into liberal arts."

It is easy to see how hard it would be to lure engineering students away from the siren of money. Not only do most poets make little money, they also have few readers. "To be a poet," Rubin said, sitting in the Emory library where he still does most of his work, "is to resign yourself to a small audience."

Although he has published three collections of poetry, the last *All My Mirrors Lie* (1975), and had poems published in *Harper's*, the *New Yorker*, the *Saturday Review*, and many other magazines, Rubin says he could count the number of fan letters he's gotten "on both hands and toes." Most people who enjoy poetry, he said, "are not going to sit down and write a letter."

"Somebody once said that of publishing a poem is like dropping a rose petal down the Grand Canyon and expecting to hear a big splash." Rubin smiled. "If you expect any real reaction, don't hold your breath. You spend half your life going to the post office," he said, explaining how he gets his poems published. "I keep about thirty envelopes circulating. It's a big job just keeping records. When I first started, I got a year-and-a-half of rejection slips before I sold a poem. Now I get an average of two acceptances a month. Just because a publisher rejects a poem doesn't mean it isn't any good. You just have to trust you'll hit the right editor."

But the heartbreak of being a poet doesn't come with the rejection slips as much as with the acceptance check. Poets are hardly paid at all. "If I make $200 a year out of publishing poems," Rubin said with a slight, quizzical smile, "I figure it's been a good year."

# James Seay

James Seay, like many other writers, can go to his bookshelves and find the book that first sparked for him an interest in literature. "It's somewhere in here," Seay told me, running his fingers past a shelf of titles. "Here it is," he said, with a satisfied look on his face, "the Pocket Book edition of *Modern American Short Stories.*" Seay flipped through the pages, finally coming to a William Faulkner story, "That Evening Sun Go Down." The story, which had various scribblings along the margins and between paragraphs, had obviously been read more than once.

Seay, a Mississippi native, was not aware of Faulkner until he read that story. He said he was living in Florida at the time, and the story took him back to his own Mississippi landscape and culture in a magical way. "The book I wish were here," he said with a broad smile on his face, "is one my uncle sent me from Marshall Field in Chicago when I was young. It was a beautiful slipcased edition of *Tom Sawyer.* I just loved that book as a kid. I would feign illness and stay in bed to read it. I don't know how many times I read that book."

Seay, now on the faculty of the University of North Carolina at Chapel Hill, is the author of two books of poems, *Let Not Your Heart* and *Water Tables.* His first poetry was written while he was working on construction jobs in Oxford, Mississippi, after he'd dropped out of Mercer University for a few years. "Nothing that I wrote during that time has survived," Seay said, smiling. "It was really wretched poetry. Poems about bulldozers going up against magnolias and the like."

Seay returned to the University of Mississippi and then got his M.A. at the University of Virginia. Besides his two books, he has written essays and articles for numerous national and scholarly magazines. "I've never had much motivation to write prose fiction until lately. The prose I'm working on now you could call half-fiction, I guess. I don't know what it will be when it's finished."

Later, sitting on Seay's back porch, I asked him if he thought the storytelling tradition of the South had anything to do with his decision to become a writer. He looked up at the sun filtering through the tall oaks and pines in his backyard and smiled. "I'll tell you the truth," he said, "I don't remember any particular stories from my youth. That's something that you always hear, the 'storytelling tradition,' but I'm not sure we remember specific stories. Probably it's just the echo of language we remember. I remember people sitting on the porch like you and I are doing now and rocking and talking, but the stories I actually recall are from my adult life.

"In fact, my mother just recently told me a good story. My grandfather, her father, was sitting on the porch one afternoon like this and was accidentally shot in the ankle by a ricochet bullet. The sheriff, who happened to be a neighbor and good friend, was shooting at a mad dog on the railroad tracks and the bullet ricocheted and hit my grandfather. The upshot, as it were, was that the sheriff came running to take him to the doctor and actually started crying. Something no other sheriff has ever done in public, to my knowledge," Seay said, laughing. "Now that I think about it, that story was probably told within my hearing scores of times when I was young. I guess the difference is that back then I probably wanted to know how much it hurt my grandfather, whereas now I'm more interested in how much it hurt the sheriff."

# Mary Lee Settle

Mary Lee Settle has been, among other things, a New York model, an assistant editor at *Harper's Bazaar,* a free-lance journalist in London, an R.A.F. servicewoman, an expatriate, a two-time Guggenheim recipient, and a National Book Award–winner. She is a tough-minded writer whose slight English accent makes her an elegant and confident conversationalist.

Settle met me at the University of Virginia at Charlottesville where she was attending the first P.E.N.-Faulkner awards in 1981. When we finally sat down on the porch of the Colonnade Club overlooking the green designed by Thomas Jefferson, I asked, in light of all her travels, what she considered her home.

"If someone asked me where I was *from,"* she said, looking out across the lawn, "I'd say that I didn't know. I was born in West Virginia and got out as soon as possible. I have lived in London more than I have in West Virginia."

Settle, who now lives in Norfolk, Virginia, said she does not have much nostalgia for her birthplace. Although her first two novels, *The Love Eaters* (1954) and *The Kiss of Kin* (1955), had completely Southern settings, her subsequent novels have had both international and West Virginia settings.

"What I'm talking about," she said, "is growing up, leaving the place where you were brought up, finding out something in the world beyond that, and instead of being constantly concerned with the nostalgia you look around the real world and you write about it. That's why I always deny being a Southern writer."

Settle's 1977 novel *Blood Tie* won the National Book Award, much to the amazement of some critics who described her as an "unknown." She did not seem bitter about the reaction, but seemed more amused than anything else. "All that crap about me being America's neglected writer is simply not true," she said. "I haven't been neglected. For a long time I was actively suppressed. The writing community knew me and always had. I'd already been famous once and forgotten. I just got famous again. Like many other so-called Southern writers, I got caught in a critical backlash." There was a time in the early 1960s, Settle said, "when Southern writers could publish laundry lists and everybody thought it was wonderful. Then afterwards everybody who'd been good suddenly got bad and all the ones who'd been bad suddenly got good. It's all so stupid," she said, laughing.

Settle smiled and relaxed in her director's chair, cupping her chin in her palm. She looked at me as if to get in the final word. "If I thought that one line of one page of one book of my career was dependent on any critic on earth, I'd shoot myself."

# Lee Smith

A neighbor of Lee Smith's ran into the living room where Smith was being photographed. "Lee," she said, out of breath and now with an embarrassed look on her face, "I thought you had a fire, but now I see it's just the flash. I'm glad I didn't call the fire department."

Smith laughed and reassured her neighbor that everything was OK. I asked her if her neighbor knew why anyone would want to photograph Lee Smith? "Probably not," Smith said, "we don't really talk about what we do. I'd rather just be a normal person who writes novels."

Smith, like Anne Tyler, views the writing of novels as completely separate from her family life. She and her two children live in a solid middle-class neighborhood in Chapel Hill, North Carolina. There were implements of adolescent war lying around her house, bicycles crushing holly bushes at the front door, and the usual confusion of two boys raiding the refrigerator. It was hard to imagine anyone writing in the middle of all this confusion, plus keeping a full-time teaching job at North Carolina State University in Raleigh.

"I just write between it all," Smith said, directing one of her children out of camera range. "I have usually thought about a novel so long that I'm ready to write it by the time I get to my desk." She said she does more revision now, although "I used to say that I didn't revise much."

Born in the small Appalachian coal-mining town of Grundy, Virginia, Smith still speaks with a heavy Southern accent. She is a very funny woman who used to be a cheerleader. Even though Smith said she does not write didactically, she does have a point to her fiction that is sometimes hidden by the humor. "Southern women," she said, "are always trying to fit themselves into an image and trying to find the proper way to act. I mean, *Black Mountain Breakdown* is all about the dangers of this passivity."

Like many fiction writers, Smith worked for a time as a newspaper reporter. One of her novels, *Fancy Strut* (1973), was based loosely on the Tuscaloosa Sesquicentennial celebration which she covered for the *Tuscaloosa News*. But she had to give up working around newspapers and print shops because "it turned out that I was allergic to printers' ink," she told me, laughing.

Smith, who has a way of surprising an interviewer with the unexpected, told me she had a birthday coming up. I expressed sympathy for the usually tragic fortieth birthday. Smith laughed and got down off her duck-table seat. "Goodness," she said, "I'm glad about turning forty. I've been feeling like I was forty since I was twenty-five. I'm ready for forty."

# Elizabeth Spencer

Elizabeth Spencer spoke in her quiet, sophisticated Mississippi accent as she pointed out landmarks along Peachtree Street in Atlanta, where she was to speak at the South Atlantic Modern Language Association's annual meeting. "Goodness," she said, "I remember Peachtree as low houses, big trees, and small businesses. It sure has changed."

Spencer and I were driving to the Swan House off Paces Ferry Road. Although she moved to Canada with her husband in 1958, she said her heart was still in the South. "I don't think that it's entirely good to have moved to Canada," she said. "I've been personally very happy there, but as far as my work is concerned there may have been other places it might have flourished more."

Spencer, who lived in Rome on a Guggenheim Fellowship in the 1950s, said she "just barely missed being a person who lived in Europe. I used to know writers in Rome who said they wouldn't learn Italian because it would ruin their style. It doesn't even ruin your accent, let alone your style," she said, laughing.

Although Canada has never inspired her to write, Spencer said that being away from a place can help a writer. "Memory helps more than anything else in the world," she said. "When memories get very sharp, I'm apt to write about Italy, even though I'm not there. But if it goes on too long, the outlines blur."

The memory of the South has always been sharp for Spencer. Except for three books set in Europe, all her books have Southern settings. She said she returns to the South frequently, but still regrets she has had to catch the changing South "on the run."

Spencer told me Eudora Welty was one of the first to take an interest in her work, when she was a student at Belhaven College in Jackson, Mississippi. But she said she did not get serious about writing until after working a year for the *Nashville Tennessean*. "I decided that I either had to quit this newspaper nonsense and get a novel finished, rejected, or accepted or settle down and marry somebody. I quit my job and lived on a pittance and wrote every day."

Spencer was lucky, though. Donald Davidson, who had been one of her teachers at Vanderbilt, where she got her M.A., gave her manuscript to an editor-friend who offered her a contract on her first novel, *Fire in the Morning* (1948). Her second novel, *This Crooked Way* (1952), brought her the Guggenheim and the opportunity to spend some time in Italy.

"You think journalism is good for a young writer?" I asked. "It's good for writers who are a bit literary," Spencer said, smiling, "because it sharpens your style. You have to get it down quick. It's awfully good for people used to dawdling around doing poetry."

# Jesse Stuart

Jesse Stuart was recovering from his second stroke when I photographed him in May 1981. His daily routine included forty-five minutes in a wheelchair and the smoking of a single cigar.

Greenup, Kentucky, in the extreme northeast corner of the state, had been Stuart's lifelong home and the fountainhead of his fiction. The lush, mountainous countryside had inspired the share-cropper's son to write novels, stories, poems, and hundreds of essays and magazine articles about the land he loved. He was a fanatical chronicler of his own life and experiences.

Stuart lived in W-Hollow, so named for the shape of the valley creek, off a meandering road in a green two-story log cabin mortared in white and backed up against the side of a mountain. Inside, the low ceilings and exposed beams of Stuart's study made movement for a tall person seem a hazard without proper caution.

Stuart had nearly died of a heart attack in 1973 and had been fighting the condition ever since. Although the second stroke had paralyzed the left side of his body, he was enthusiastic about being photographed and not at all self-conscious. In the dappled light of the backyard Stuart savored each puff of his cigar. "What do you know, Naomi," he said to his wife of forty years when he noticed an early white blossom of an apple tree, "I think I see a bloom on one of our trees." He went on to give a short lecture on the oaks, poplars, dog-woods, and flowers of his Kentucky home.

Stuart's energy and faculties were amazing and he talked about other books that he planned to write. From his first book, *Harvest of Youth* (1930), to his last novel, *Land Beyond the River* (1973), he had been like a locomotive steaming through thousands of pages. (As I write this, I remember something Flannery O'Connor once said about him. "Jesse Stuart's ego," she wrote a friend, "was like the light on the front of a train but as Warren remarked, we probably all have that much but just know how to keep it under cover better.")

Before he married Naomi in 1940, he had written the 143,000-word *Trees of Heaven* in seventy-five days. He took the manuscript to his publisher in New York and waited until his editor called to say she would publish the book. With that advance money, he and Naomi planned their marriage.

Stuart suddenly seemed tired and asked to be taken back to bed. Naomi took me around the grounds of the house and eventually we ended up in Stuart's upstairs study. She said he had not been there for years because he could not climb the spiral staircase, but what he left behind was a testament to a lifetime of work. Bookshelf after bookshelf was lined with manuscripts. "Are these manuscripts of all the books Jesse has written?" I asked. "Yes," she said, "except for that shelf over there. Those are still unpublished works."

Jesse Stuart died February 17, 1984.

# William Styron

William Styron shuffled down the hall of the Atlanta Biltmore Hotel. He looked as if each step was a struggle, and when he reached his door he breathed a sigh of relief, glad to be home. When I interrupted his contentment, he seemed annoyed at first, but, remembering his promise earlier in the day, said, "Oh, you want to take my picture. Well, you'll have to make it snappy. I've got to get some rest."

Styron had told me to meet him in his suite between 3:00 and 6:00 P.M. and had added, "Just keep trying my number until you reach me." I had decided to wait for him, but neglected to bring anything to read, and by the time he showed up I understood the strategy of the Gideons placing Bibles in hotel rooms.

Styron said he'd been out with friends the night before and had seen very little of his bed. Despite his fatigue, he was cooperative and even good-humored. "You want me to jump up and down or stand on my head?" he said, laughing. "That seems to be what most photographers want me to do these days." I asked him to sit in front of the mirror.

What is surprising about Styron is the attention that has been given a writer who had produced only four novels, one novella, and a play in thirty-three years. His first novel, *Lie Down in Darkness* (1951), written when he was only twenty-six, won the Prix de Rome, and his third, *The Confessions of Nat Turner* (1967), won a Pulitzer Prize. His fourth novel, *Sophie's Choice* (1979), had just been published a few months before to enthusiastic critical and popular acclaim.

Styron, a native Virginian, was at first hesitant about being included in a book of Southern writers, though all of his books have either a Southern setting or a Southern protagonist. He said he did not see himself as a writer like Eudora Welty or Flannery O'Connor, who are closely identified with the South. That is, he explained, he was Southern in his "biases and sympathies," but "my work is not strongly regional."

Styron sat on the corner of a narrow table under the mirror, staring blankly at the camera. After fewer than twenty frames, he stood up and said, "Have you got enough?" I nodded as if twenty frames is usually my limit.

Instead of asking me to leave, which would have been impolite and not in keeping with Southern sensibilities, he invited me to stay for a drink. At the time, the movie rights to *Sophie's Choice* had been sold and Alan Pakula had agreed to write and direct the film. Styron said he didn't want to write the script because he felt "that was old ground" and he wanted to move on to another book, *The Way of the Warrior*.

"Which reminds me," he said, getting out of his chair and rubbing his face, "I've got to get some work done today, but before I can do that, I've got to get some sleep." He shook my hand, thanked me for coming, and shuffled back to his room and closed the door.

# Peter Taylor

Peter Taylor stood in front of a plantation-sized painting of his grandfather. He spoke in his refined Southern accent about the history of the Taylor family, cupping his hands together as if a tour guide. "All of them were landowners and in politics, you know, and he was a literate man," Taylor said, pointing to the painting. "They all had literary pretensions and interests. My grandfather for several years edited a magazine called the *Trotwood-Taylor Magazine* in Nashville and was later in the Senate after running against his brother.

"Well," he added with a smile as if boring his audience, "they're all interesting to me, but I don't know that your family history is interesting to everybody. Your garden and your family history are things nobody else is interested in."

Taylor, who lives in Charlottesville, Virginia, is the author of nine books, including *A Long Fourth* (1948) and several other short story collections. His stories appear frequently in the *New Yorker*. But despite his success, Taylor does not see himself as a professional writer.

"I mean it in this sense," he said. "I think that professionalism is carelessly close to commercialism and a professional writer has to have a book out every year. I think there's such a thing as waiting for inspiration. As soon as an artist becomes a professional man, that's like being a lawyer or a doctor and that's not the same thing as being an artist."

It would seem that Taylor had little choice in the direction of his life, even without his heritage. His roommate in college was Robert Lowell, and his teachers at Southwestern in Memphis and Vanderbilt in Nashville included Allen Tate, John Crowe Ransom, and Donald Davidson. His teacher at Southwestern, Tate, is reported to have said he couldn't teach Taylor anything about writing. "Well, he's said to have said that," Taylor told me, laughing, "but I was a precocious young writer. I don't know if I've gotten any better or not."

Taylor and Tate became lifelong friends, and Taylor eventually married Eleanor Ross, who was another of Tate's students. Now both Eleanor, a poet, and Taylor write every day in the shadow of Taylor's ancestors—Eleanor upstairs and Taylor downstairs.

But, Taylor said, he doesn't like to spend all his time around writers. Even when he owned a house in Key West, he said, he saw few writers, including the city's most famous resident, Tennessee Williams. "I met him," Taylor said, "but I found him rather hard to talk with about anything except his plays. He was very interesting on that subject."

Taylor, who has two children, said he didn't discourage them from becoming writers but he did warn them of the pitfalls. "I used to say there were no great father-and-offspring teams," he said, "when I did try to warn them. Then I thought to myself, maybe someday people will say, 'Did you know that Katy Taylor's father once wrote some stories?'"

# Anne Tyler

Anne Tyler does not give interviews, do talk shows, deliver lectures, or teach writing classes. Tyler does not refuse because she wants to be difficult or to create a reclusive persona like J. D. Salinger. She is genuinely a private person who had rather the public not be part of her personal life.

"Interviews just seem beside the point," she said as her thirteen-year-old cat Sesame hopped in her lap, "and it's not that I didn't try them. But they would always take inordinate amounts of time and they would always be embarrassing to read. Once I said I didn't want to do interviews," she said, "it was easier to say no to everybody. It simplified life a lot. I know writers who do a lot of interviews and I don't know how they get any work done."

Tyler has been able to get a good deal of work done in the past eighteen years. Besides raising two daughters, she has written nine novels. Her last, *Dinner at the Homesick Restaurant* (1982), was on the *New York Times* best-seller list for months and got considerable review attention in the press.

Tyler said she does a lot of reviews herself. "But," she said, laughing, "that seems like some other self of mine. A nice side effect of being a writer is that after a few years it's amazing how many things arrive at your door to read. I used to cost my husband a lot of money for books. Now, I practically don't have to buy books."

Talking with Tyler is like reading one of her books. There is a familiarity and comfort in the conversation. I found myself talking about family matters and personal relationships as if I'd known her for years. Tyler, too, talks very candidly about her family. However, her work is another matter. "I'll have to show it to my agent," she said when asked about her new book, "to see if it's any good."

Although she was born in Minneapolis, Tyler grew up in the South. She attended Duke University, where she was the first student to sign up for an English class under Reynolds Price, a new faculty member. Her books for the most part are set in Maryland, but many characters have Southern backgrounds.

"I'm really not a Southern writer," she said. "I feel like it's presumptuous in a way because I had a Northern family. I grew up in the South, but I always looked enviously at Southern families and wished I could be a part of one of them."

# Margaret Walker

Finding where Margaret Walker lives in Jackson, Mississippi, is a simple matter. Once you get in her neighborhood, you just look around for a new sign that says Margaret Walker Alexander Drive. Finding her at home is another matter. "I've been retired for five years and I've worked harder than ever," she told me.

Margaret Walker, best known for her novel *Jubilee* (1967), is indeed a remarkable woman. It would have been hard enough growing up in the pre- and post-Depression South as a white person, but Walker seemed to flourish in a depressed and racist society. "I went to school at age five," she said in her articulate and measured sentences, "but mother taught me to read when I was four. I do not, in fact, remember a time when I could not read."

Walker finished Northwestern University when she was barely twenty, and eventually got an M.A. and then a Ph.D. from the University of Iowa. In 1937 she wrote *For My People,* a daring book of poems that was published five years later and that influenced many other black writers. John Oliver Killens calls her "one of the greatest influences on my life."

Although Walker spent almost four years working for the WPA in Chicago, she has lived most of her life in the South. "I was born in Alabama, 250 miles from here," she said, "I grew up in New Orleans, 200 miles from here, and went to school in Meridian, 90 miles from here, so this is the epicenter of my life."

Walker spent thirty of her seventy years teaching at Jackson State University, writing books, and working for civil rights. I asked her how she thought the South had changed over those years. She answered the question in parts between talking on the phone, responding to her secretary's questions about a manuscript, and answering the door.

"The South has changed in a dozen different ways," she said. "The main change was in race relations. The civil rights movement was a revolution in the South. Black people underwent two kinds of revolutions: the Negro revolution led by Martin Luther King and the black revolution led by Malcolm X. It took away forever the slave mentality and forced the white South to change its political stance. It was also very good for business," she said, smiling now, "because it opened up society."

I asked her about her father, whom she credits with her love of books. "He was a preacher, an educator, and a scholar," she said. "I never met anyone who knew ancient history or the Bible as well. He was not a typical Southern fundamentalist, though. He taught me to read the Bible as you would any world literature, as symbolic.

"But, most important, he taught me the importance of reading. Reading is the most essential thing for a writer," she said, giving the formula with appropriate pauses. "Thinking first, reading next, then the writing follows."

# Robert Penn Warren

"I'd like to make a few changes here," Robert Penn Warren said as he leafed through my copy of *A Place to Come To*. "This is a different edition than mine, so I'll have to look it up."

I told him I didn't mind waiting and sat on top of a stack of books, papers, and manuscripts in his Fairfield, Connecticut, office. Warren compared pages of his corrected edition with mine, adding a comma, semicolon, or an occasional word. He made the changes so carefully that I had to read the entire book again just to find the corrected pages.

Earlier I had told Warren that *A Place to Come To* was one of my favorite novels, running a close second to *All the Kings Men*. He smiled and said mischievously, "Yes, you know I just reread that book and I find that it's a pretty damn fine book."

Born in Guthrie, Kentucky, in 1905, Warren has published more than thirty-five books since he began his writing career at Vanderbilt in the early twenties under the tutelage of John Crowe Ransom. He was one of the original members of the Fugitives, along with Ransom, Allen Tate, and Donald Davidson. He is the only writer to have ever won the Pulitzer Prize for both fiction (*All the King's Men,* 1947) and poetry (*Promises,* 1958).

When I photographed him in 1982, Warren did not appear to be a man nearly eighty. His energy and enthusiasm seemed boundless. He led me into a sitting room overlooking the stark, leafless Connecticut countryside and poured out two bourbons. He handed me one and with his free hand threw a heavy dumbbell off a rocker and sat down.

He apologized for putting me off nearly two years. "I treated you shabbily," he said, "and even the whip and chain I've been under can scarcely excuse me." He walked over to a sideboard and brought a picture of him and Eleanor Clark, his novelist wife, sitting on camels in Egypt, giving that as one of the reasons for the delay. "It was quite a harrowing way to travel," he said, laughing.

Warren still writes every day from 9:30 A.M. until 2:00 P.M. He and his wife make the short walk from their house to the converted tack and equipment rooms of the adjacent barn each morning. Eleanor stops at the first orderly, well-lit office and Warren walks past an open stable to his workplace, a room most accurately described as disheveled.

Rummaging behind the desk, he looked like an elderly small-town newspaper editor looking for his weekly budget. He found a copy of *All the King's Men,* not the book he was looking for, and I asked to see it. Thumbing through the yellowing pages, I admitted to reading the book at least ten times—maybe more.

He stopped what he was doing and stood up, an astounded look coming across his face. "My God, ten times," he said, laughing now in the legendary Red Warren fashion. "That must be some kind of record."

# Eudora Welty

Eudora Welty drove me back to the Holiday Inn in a maroon Cutlass Supreme with a five-speed Hurst speed-shifter on the floor. She ran through the gears with great precision, all the while pointing out Jackson, Mississippi, landmarks.

"Did you order this car special?" I asked. "Oh, no!" Welty said, laughing, almost embarrassed. "I just went out to the Oldsmobile place and bought the only car they had with a straight drive. I like the feeling that I'm doing the driving, not an automatic shift."

As she drove away from the hotel, popping second and giving the oncoming traffic a fleeting but perfectly cognizant glance, I could not help but hum a familiar Beach Boys song.

At seventy-five, Welty is the superstar of Southern literature. Her reputation as a major voice in contemporary American literature has always been secure with critics, but in recent years she has achieved the mixed blessing of celebrity. She gets many requests to speak, teach, be interviewed or photographed, write or be written about. For many writers, the enormous attention could be damaging to their work and perspective, but Welty seems oblivious to the fact that she has become incredibly famous for a serious writer. She remains a genteel Southern lady.

Welty was born in Jackson in 1909 and still lives in the house her father built in 1925. Its Tudor style is unassuming and straightforward like her stories. She does not have walls lined with awards, honors, and degrees, or photographs of herself accepting them. They would be out of character.

"You're not going to plug anything in, are you?" she asked as I set up. "The last time I had some photographers here, they blew all my fuses."

We sat in her library for a while talking about writers and eventually taking pictures. I handed her a camera and she seemed glad to hold it. "Did you ever want to be just a photographer?" I asked, recalling her days as a WPA photographer. "Goodness, no!" she said, handing the camera back. "I never started out to be a photographer. I always wanted to write. Taking pictures was part of my job, and I loved it, but my real work and real love was writing."

# James Whitehead

A fair number of James Whitehead's seven children and their friends were milling about his home in Fayetteville, Arkansas, and probably making unpardonable messes in the kitchen. The scene at first looked like a teenage day camp, and I could not imagine a writer working under these conditions. But Whitehead said he had no problem working at home. "I just go in my office, lock the door, and don't come out until I want to."

Whitehead's description of his working habits is probably true and it is doubtful if any of his children or their guests would question his edicts. He is an imposing figure and, like his fictional character Sonny Joiner from his novel *Joiner* (1971), not someone you'd want to cross.

Although Whitehead's tough exterior is at least partly a result of his days playing football in high school and at Vanderbilt, he is not someone who revels in the past days on the field. "I enjoyed playing football," he said. "But the real importance of football was finally that it gave me the opportunity to go to Vanderbilt."

Whitehead grew up in Jackson, Mississippi, the hometown of Alice Walker, Margaret Walker, Beth Henley, and Eudora Welty. He said he had no explanation for why so many writers come from Mississippi. "I really don't understand it," he said after locking himself in his study, "but I'm not sure if it's all that good to realize that the best writer in the world, Eudora Welty, lives in the town you grew up in. But when you get down to it, I like it just fine."

Fayetteville, the university town where Whitehead teaches and his home for the last twenty years, has more than its share of writers. "For a small town," Whitehead said, talking a puff of his cigarette, "you're not going to find more writers than in this one. At one time there were something like six or eight novelists living within three miles of me."

Whitehead looked behind him and found a few of his neighbors' books. He ran across a copy of *Local Men,* a book of his poems published in 1979, and *Domains,* his first collection of poems, published in 1966, and signed them. "I want you to have these," he said, "because you came a long way to take my picture."

Despite his imposing exterior, Whitehead is a sensitive and generous poet. His first book of poems was highly influenced by his aversion to racism.

A knock brought Whitehead to his feet. "Yes?" he said firmly. "Telephone," said a voice through the door. When he returned he was smiling. Gen, his wife, had gone to the hospital that week for medical tests and they had proved negative. Surprised that the worry had not shown in his face, I asked him if writers handle adversity better than most people and if that helps them write.

"Probably," he said. "It contributes to everything. I can't imagine any kind of successful life without having to prove yourself. You have to push against something. A smooth life," he said, emphasizing the last word, "I suspect would be a smooth slide."

# Sylvia Wilkinson

Sylvia Wilkinson greeted me at the door of her sister's house in Chapel Hill, North Carolina, holding a large cat that looked to be a mixture of Persian and alley cat. "This is Sally O'Malley," she said, putting the animal down with three other cats milling about the floor of her sister's studio.

"It's embarrassing," she said. "We have thirteen cats—three in California and ten here. We used to laugh when we'd hear stories of little old ladies dying and relatives finding two hundred cats inside. But let me tell you, it could happen."

Wilkinson, who grew up in Durham, North Carolina, has been a California resident off and on for the past fifteen years. She is a prolific writer who divides her time between being a novelist, a journalist, and a timer for some of the best professional car racing teams in the country. Wilkinson said she picked up the timing skill over a period of years and eventually became the timer for Paul Newman's racing team. "I could make a profession of it," she said, laughing, "but I time to support my writing habit."

Wilkinson tried to explain what a timer's job is on a racing team. "It's highly intense work," she said, "but for me it's better than teaching. Teaching is a very creative business. Timing doesn't require any creativity whatsoever. When I leave the racing scene, I don't have the kind of exhaustion I did in the academic world. Besides," she added with a laugh, "I like it greasy, noisy, and dirty."

Wilkinson said she does not advertise the fact that she's a writer at the racetrack. "Some of the crew know I'm a writer," she said, "but they don't care. The women at the track read the kind of novels with the tinfoil writing on the cover and women in long dresses. They read the successful stuff, not the stuff I write."

Besides her five novels, Wilkinson has written three books of nonfiction and fifteen juvenile books including a series under the name of Eric Speed. But despite her outward irreverence toward her own work, she says she is a serious writer who would rather take her seriousness in doses.

"I like to see other writers now and then," she said, picking up Sally O'Malley again, suddenly serious for the first time all afternoon, "but I don't want to be in that environment all the time. My work is serious and that's enough seriousness and intellectualism for me."

"You plan to stay in California, then?" I asked. "I don't make any plans," she said, laughing again. "I know I'm glad that I didn't grow up in Los Angeles because it doesn't have any weather. As my grandmother would say, 'If you grow up in a place without any weather, you grow up without any character.'"

# Jonathan Williams

Jonathan Williams stood with folded arms in his Highlands, North Carolina, retreat. He pointed in a northward direction and continued to denigrate the developers of his pristine Blue Ridge Mountains. "Sky Valley is the southernmost ski resort in North America," Williams said with a smile. "It used to be called Mud Creek. When they finish developing, most of what there is to see—the trees, shrubs, and plants—will be gone."

Williams is by no means a recluse. He is a poet who regularly gives readings (over a thousand) and lectures and who occasionally takes a poet-in-residence assignment from a university. Williams's problem with the development of Highlands is his aversion to being in the middle of any trend, whether it's real estate or literature.

He has made his reputation by remaining on the outside of established publishing methods and subjects. Witness the titles of some of his books: *Polycotyledonous Poems* (1967), *Lullabies Twisters Gibbers Drags* (1963), and *Descant on Rawthey's Madrigal* (1968). In 1951 he established the Jargon Society, a nonprofit publishing company dedicated to outsiders of the literary and visual arts fields. Besides Williams's seven collections of poetry and prose published by traditional publishing houses, he has published some eighty books, pamphlets, and broadsides through the underground press.

"I don't want to play the New York game," he told me, "and if you live in the places I do, they're not going to come to you. I've always been cranky, like all mountain people. I like to do things my own way."

Williams's educational career was also an exercise in self-expression. Although he attended Princeton for a time, he never got a formal degree. After dropping out of Princeton, he studied painting with Karl Knaths in Washington, D.C., and etching and engraving with Stanley William Hayter in New York. In 1951 he returned to North Carolina, where he was born in 1929, to attend Black Mountain College, a school that offered no degree.

Williams said his tendency to associate with and publish the work of artists some people would call "eccentric or wacko" has kept him out of the academic culture of the South. "I get along better with pileated woodpeckers, galax leaves, and rattlesnakes than I do with Senator Helms, professors, 'poetry lovers,' and tire salesmen."

"Down South," Williams said, puffing on his cigar and staring intently at the camera, "people tend to divide other people into those who are common and those who are nice. I don't write for either one. I write for people who like to read what I write."

# Miller Williams

"There's a strange honesty about country music," Miller Williams told me, looking at a picture of his friend Tom T. Hall. "It's nearly always about our lives after we're grown up and married and the hard edges of those lives. Pop music is generally about idealized love—hardly anyone in a pop or rock song is married."

Tom T. is one of many of his friends—country music stars and fiction writers and poets—hanging on the walls of Williams's study in Fayetteville, Arkansas: Johnny Cash, George Jones, Isaac Asimov, Richard Hugo, Donald Justice, Flannery O'Connor, John Ciardi. The four walls are covered with them. "I like to have my friends around me when I work," he explained.

Williams, who was born in Hoxie, Arkansas, and has spent most of his life in his native state, didn't start out to be a poet. He was a professor of biology and a researcher for ten years before leaving the field of science to devote most of his energies to his writing.

Since his first book of poems, *A Circle of Stone,* published in 1964, Williams has published five other collections. He has also been a Fulbright professor at the University of Mexico, visiting professor at the University of Chile, and spent a year in Rome at the American Academy.

Williams said he discovered he had a facility for language and translation during his travels and has since translated books by the Spanish poet Nicanor Parra and the Italian poet Giuseppe Belli. "I would read a poem and want to show it to my friends," he said, explaining how he got interested in translation "and the only way that I could do that was to translate it."

"I didn't decide to be a poet," Williams told me later, sitting at his cribbage board shuffling cards. "I just realized that most of my publications were in the field of letters and so I finally came out of the closet and began teaching English at LSU." Now, as director of the University of Arkansas Press, he teaches occasionally at the university, publishes other people's books, and writes his own.

Although he likes the Southern hills and wouldn't live anywhere else (outside of Rome), he doesn't like to be thought of as a Southern poet. "I'm a Southerner and I'm a poet," he said. "Those two facts complement one another in some good ways, but neither has to proscribe the other."

Williams said that city life seemed to get on his nerves and that he liked living in the Ozarks. "It's quiet, the air is clean, and I have a lot of good friends here. Besides," he said, putting the cards down, "I have to hear the scratch of my fountain pen on paper to write."

## Tennessee Williams

When Tennessee Williams first spoke to me from a bed hidden somewhere in the darkness of his Key West bedroom, all the confidence I had rallied walking up to his Duncan Street bungalow left me like a spirit. "I want a picture in the dark," he said with theatrical precision. "Can you do that?"

"Sure," I said in an unsteady voice. "Do you want a profile or a full face?"

Williams laughed and told John, his *GQ*-looking companion who had opened the door for me, to turn on the light. I heard John feel his way along the wall and then a click. There sat Williams in the middle of his bed, his hair in tangles and a gnomic smile on his face. He looked very much like one of the seven dwarfs gone bad.

"I want a picture of me in bed," he said, lying down and pulling the covers up to his chin. He sat up straight and said, laughing, "John, my Queen! Bring me my Queen!" John came back with a large Boston bull. "Now, take my picture," Williams said. "The queen with his Queen."

Williams's ability to make jokes about anything, including his homosexuality, made what otherwise might have been an awkward day a delight. When we were sitting outside in the gazebo drinking wine after I had run out of film, I told him about a particularly attractive blond I'd seen the night before in a bar. He smiled and said with a touch of irony, "So you like women? Well, I used to have that weakness too."

Williams showed me the manuscript of his latest play, *Clothes for a Summer Hotel,* which was produced in 1980. He said he was leaving Key West the next day to see to its production. Williams seemed so excited about the play, one would have thought it his first. According to him, it was his first play. "I do not remember writing *Streetcar* or *Glass Menagerie,*" he said. "I did that a long time ago. The most important work for me is the work I'm doing now."

I asked for a second day of shooting, but Williams declined, saying that he was going to New York the next day to see his agent.

Four years later I called to ask if I could update my photograph, but no one answered. The next day I learned why. Tennessee Williams was in New York again, but dead at the age of seventy-one in a lower East Side hotel room.